Book of Mormon Stories

for Young Latter-day Saints

Emma Marr Petersen

BOOKCRAFT
Salt Lake City, Utah

Contents

Contents

(Continued)

Contents

(Continued)

Illustrations

Foreword

A short time ago a friend of mine, the mother of a nine-year-old son, bemoaned the fact that on a certain day each week she had to go to the nearby drugstore and forcibly bring home her youngster; for that was the day on which the new funny-books were brought for sale. This child stopped there on his way home from school and stayed to read all of them until interrupted by one of his parents, regardless of time!

Yes, our children are well supplied with literature of a certain type. These books are plentiful, cheap, and sensational. Youngsters give their parents little trouble while reading them. But what ideals are they forming in these their most impressionable years? What standards of behavior do these so-called comic books encourage?

It was for children of this type that Book of Mormon stories were prepared. The heroes are just as courageous, the situations just as thrilling, the drama as tense as in any work of fiction. But these stories are true, and truth is all-powerful. The Book of Mormon was originally written for the purpose of bringing conversion to young as well as to old. This idea is expressed in Second Nephi, verse twenty-three: "For we labor diligently to write, to persuade our children, and also our brethren, to believe in Christ, and to be reconciled to God; for we know that it is by grace that we are saved, after all we can do."

In this busy Church of ours, much of the work in the auxiliaries is done by young mothers, whose multitudinous duties prevent them from having time to simplify and condense Book of Mormon incidents to suit the capacity and interest of young children. We hope that they will be used by this group also.

Many mothers have written asking for such a book after having read the "Bible Stories for Young Latter-day Saints." They would like to discourage their young ones in their use of the comic book stories, but feel they have little to replace them.

These Book of Mormon incidents occurred in our own land of America, and some of the traditions discussed in school may be confirmed by this volume. The stories are simple and concise, and may be read and understood by young children.

We hope they will read them, and as did one of the Presidents of our Church in recent years, model their lives from the heroes who lived in our country so many years ago.

EMMA MARR PETERSEN

CHAPTER ONE

The Promised Land

Genesis 6-9; Ether 1.

*T*HE LAND of America is greatly loved by the Lord. He has called it the Promised Land for many years, and has told us that it is the choicest land in all the world.

It was on this side of the world where Noah built his ark before the flood. Noah preached to his neighbors for 120 years telling them that unless they repented the Lord would send a flood to drown them.

They did not repent, so the Lord told Noah to take his family into the ark he had built, and to take animals and seeds of all kinds also. When he had done this the floods began. Rain poured down upon the earth for forty days, fountains and springs adding to the torrents. It was not long until even the highest mountain tops were covered with water. All of the people and the animals on earth were drowned excepting those who were with Noah.

The ark floated on the waters for five months, drifting half-way around the world. At last it came to rest on top of a high mountain named Ararat near the land of Palestine. After three months, the tops of the mountains began to appear, as the waters went down. It was not until four more months had passed that Noah and his family and all the animals could leave the ark.

Noah and his wife had three sons, Shem, Ham and Japheth, whose wives also were with them in the ark. When the flood was over, and they started life on the earth once more, children were born to them. As their families grew in numbers, they began to spread out over the land, forming villages and little towns of their own.

1

. . The Lord touches the stones with his finger

Years passed, and the people continued to increase until they became very numerous. As they worked, building cities and working on farms, they became wealthy, and some of them again became wicked. One group decided to build a large city, and in it a high tower which they hoped would reach to heaven. This greatly displeased the Lord. He went down to where they were building the tower, and confused the language of the people, so they could not understand one another. Because they all spoke different languages, they stopped work on the tower. Many of them with their families, moved to other parts of that country where they made their homes.

A righteous man named Jared lived near the tower at this time. He had a brother who was large and very strong, whom the Lord loved because he was faithful. Jared told his brother to pray that the language of their families might not be changed. He did so, and the Lord heard and answered his prayer.

Jared sent his brother again to ask the Lord whether they also should leave that part of the country as many others were doing since their language had been changed. If they were supposed to leave, where should they go? He said to his brother, "Who knoweth but the Lord will carry us forth into a land which is choice above all the earth? And if it so be let us be faithful unto the Lord, that we may receive it for our inheritance."

The brother of Jared went to the Lord as Jared had asked. When the Lord heard his prayer, he blessed Jared, his brother and their families, and agreed to do as Jared had said, and send them to a land which was choice above all other lands. This land was America, where Noah had lived before the flood, and which was then set apart by the Lord for those who believed on him and would serve him.

As the brother of Jared finished his prayer, the Lord said to him: "Go and gather together thy flocks, both male and female of every kind, and also of the seed of the earth of every kind, and

2

thy family, and also Jared thy brother and his family, and also thy friends and their families; and the friends of Jared and their families. And when thou hast done this thou shalt go at the head of them down into the valley which is northward. And there will I meet thee, and I will go before thee into a land which is choice above all the lands of the earth."

The Lord made a promise to them, saying, "And there will I bless thee and thy seed, and raise up unto me of thy seed, upon all the face of the earth. And thus will I do unto thee because this long time ye have cried unto me."

He planned to bring them to America.

CHAPTER TWO

The Journey Begins

*T*HE BROTHER of Jared told Jared and their friends what the Lord had commanded. They at once began to gather all of their flocks together. Traps were set to catch birds of different kinds, which they planned to take with them. They also caught fish, and put them in little vessels of water, to keep them alive during the journey. They gathered together swarms of bees also, which they called "deseret." It is from Jared and his family, that we use that name today. They also collected seeds of all kinds.

When they were ready, the brother of Jared led them all into the valley to the north, which the Lord had mentioned. It was called the valley of Nimrod, being named after a great hunter.

As they arrived in the valley, the Lord came down and met them as he had promised. He talked with the brother of Jared, but was covered by a cloud so that he could not be seen. The Lord commanded that they should travel still further from home, and go to a part of the wilderness in which men had never lived before. The Lord himself went with them, and led the way. He remained in the cloud, so that the people could not see him, but he spoke and gave directions for their journey.

After traveling in the wilderness, they came to the seashore, where they began to build boats, or barges. Eight of them were needed to carry the people, their animals, seeds and other belongings. For four years they lived on the seashore in the wilderness. The Lord continued to visit and speak to them. He told them of the Promised Land to which he was taking them, and said that it would always be a land of freedom to the righteous who lived upon it. But he said, if the people became wicked, he would destroy them. He promised that if the people who lived on that

4

choice land would serve Him, they would never be brought into captivity or bondage, nor would they ever be made slaves. This was a great promise.

The people of Jared lived in tents during the four years they were in the wilderness. While they were there, they began to forget the Lord, and the brother of Jared also forgot, and did not pray as he once did. This made the Lord angry. One day God came down from heaven and stood before the brother of Jared. Again he was in a cloud, so that he could not be seen. For three hours he talked with him rebuking him because he had forgotten to pray.

The brother of Jared was very sorry and asked for forgiveness. The Lord said, "I will forgive thee and thy brethren of their sins, but thou shalt not sin any more, for ye shall remember that my Spirit will not always strive with men." The brother of Jared was also told that if he became a wicked man he would be cut off from the presence of the Lord, who would not visit him any more.

In deep repentance, the brother of Jared prayed sincerely to the Lord for help and guidance. Having forgiven them the Lord now told them how to build the barges, or boats, so that they could cross the sea to the Promised Land. The boats were small and light upon the water, as tight as a dish, both top and bottom, so that if the waves should break over them, they would not leak. They were about as long as a large tree, and were pointed at the ends.

When the barges were finished, and the doors all closed, the brother of Jared found that it was so dark inside that no one could see. He wondered how the journey over the ocean could be made in such darkness, so he went again to the Lord in prayer, and said:

"O Lord, I have performed the work which thou hast commanded me, and I have made the barges according as thou hast directed me.

"And behold, O Lord, in them there is no light; whither shall we steer? And also we shall perish for in them we cannot breathe, save it is the air which is in them, therefore we shall perish."

The Lord told the brother of Jared to make holes in each boat to let in fresh air. Covers were made for these holes to protect the people when the barges were under water. But they still had no light. Again they prayed for help.

The Lord told them that when they crossed the ocean, they would sail on the surface of the water some of the time, like boats do today, but at other times he would take them through the water, under the surface. He said, "Ye shall be as a whale in the midst of the sea."

He asked the brother of Jared what he wanted to serve as a light in the boats, saying, "Ye cannot have windows for they will be dashed in pieces; neither shall ye take fire with you, for ye shall not go by the light of fire. * * * * Therefore, what will ye that I should prepare for you that ye may have light when ye are swallowed up in the depths of the sea?"

CHAPTER THREE

The Lord Appears

Ether 3.

*T*HE LORD wanted the brother of Jared to tell him how he would like to have the barges lighted. Knowing this, the prophet went into the hills where he found some clear stone like glass. From it he cut sixteen small pieces. Carrying them in his hands he climbed to the top of a high mountain, and there began to pray.

He asked the Lord not to be angry with him because of his weaknesses, and he prayed for mercy on all the people of Jared, who needed his help, especially now as they were about to begin their journey over the sea. Again he told the Lord they did not wish to travel in darkness. Then he said:

"Behold these things which I have molten out of the rock. I know, O Lord, that thou hast all power and can do whatsoever thou wilt for the benefit of man. Therefore, touch these stones, O Lord, with thy finger and prepare them that they may shine forth in darkness; and they shall shine forth unto us in the vessels which we have prepared, that we may have light while we shall cross the sea."

When the brother of Jared had finish praying, the Lord stretched out his hand and touched the stones one by one with his finger.

To his great surprise, the brother of Jared saw the finger of the Lord, and it looked like the finger of a mortal man. Such fear came upon him, when he saw this, that he fell to the ground.

The Lord said, "Arise. Why hast thou fallen?"

The frightened prophet replied, "I saw the finger of the Lord and I feared lest he should smite me, for I knew not that the Lord had flesh and blood."

7

The Lord who spoke to the brother of Jared was Jesus, who many years later would be born of Mary, the young Jewish maiden, here on earth and then die on the cross in the crucifixion. At the time he appeared to the brother of Jared he was still a spirit, just as we were spirits before being born into this earth. So he said to the brother of Jared:

"Because of thy faith thou hast seen that I shall take upon me flesh and blood. Never has man come before me with such exceeding faith as thou hast, for were it not so ye could not have seen my finger. Sawest thou more than this?"

The prophet said, "Nay, Lord, show thyself unto me."

The Lord said, "Believest thou the words which I shall speak?"

Jared's brother said, "Yea Lord, I know that thou speakest the truth, for thou art a God of truth, and canst not lie."

Then the Lord showed himself to the prophet. As he did so, he said, "I am Jesus Christ. * * Seest thou that ye are created after mine own image? Yea even all men were created in the beginning after mine own image. Behold this body which ye now behold is the body of my spirit, and man have I created after the body of my spirit, and even as I appear unto thee to be in the spirit, will I appear unto my people in the flesh."

It was a wonderful experience for the brother of Jared. The Lord now told him to write an account of it, but he told the prophet the record must be hidden up not to be read until Jesus came in the flesh hundreds of years later. He gave the brother of Jared two stones which were to be kept with this record. These stones would permit another prophet, who would live many years later, to read the account of this great experience. Jared would write in his own language. This other prophet who would read it would speak a different language. The two stones would be like the Urim and Thummim given to the Prophet Joseph Smith to translate the Book of Mormon. They would help him read the record of the brother of Jared.

CHAPTER FOUR

They Set Sail

Ether 6.

*T*HE STONES touched by the finger of the Lord now glowed with light. The brother of Jared took them down from the mountain, and put two of them in every boat, one at each end, and they lighted up the barges.

Now that they had light, the people of Jared began loading their possessions and making ready to sail. They took their families into the boats, also the animals, with food and water for all of them. Then they sailed into the sea, trusting to the Lord to bring them safely to the Land of Promise.

The Lord caused a strong wind to blow across the water toward the Promised Land, and so the little barges were carried over the sea. They were tossed about on the waves in the strong wind, and sometimes they were buried in the depths of the sea as high waves broke over them, so that they sailed under the water like a whale, just as the Lord had said.

The winds were so strong that they caused great storms on the ocean, but the people were perfectly safe inside their boats, which had been built so well that no water could enter. When they were under water very long, and could not get fresh air, they prayed to the Lord, and he brought them to the surface so that they could open the doors in their boats. Being thankful for the protection and blessing of the Lord, the people sang praises to him all through their journey. They were 344 days traveling across the ocean.

At last they arrived in the Promised Land, which later became known as America. When they came ashore, they knelt in humble prayer to the Lord, and with tears of joy, thanked him for his mercies to them.

They took their possessions, their animals and their seeds out of the boats, and began to make homes for themselves in this new land. They tilled the earth, and made farms. They built houses for their families, believed the commandments of the Lord, and served him. Altogether, there were twenty-two persons who made the journey.

More children were born to them in their new homes, and as the families grew larger, they moved out more and more into other parts of the land. The Lord blessed them in their crops and herds, and they prospered and were happy.

Years went by, and the Brother of Jared became an old man. One day he said to Jared: "Let us gather together our people that we may number them that we may know of them what they will desire of us before we go down to our graves."

The people were all called together into a large meeting. They were asked if they wished anything of Jared and his brother before they died. The people said they would like one of their number to be appointed as their king, to govern them. Jared and his brother were grieved to hear this, and feared it would cause trouble. The Lord had told them that the land should be free, and that none who lived on it would ever be brought into bondage as long as they lived righteously on the earth. The brother of Jared feared that a wicked king might lead the people into some form of bondage, and he said, "Surely this thing leadeth into captivity."

But Jared persuaded his brother to let the people do as they wished. At last he said, "Choose ye out from among our sons a king, even whom ye will."

The people chose the eldest son of the brother of Jared. His name was Pagag. But Pagag refused to be king. The people came to his father, and asked him to compel him to accept this position, but his father would not, telling them that they should not force any man to be their king. They chose one of Pagag's brothers, who refused also. Then they chose another, but neither would he accept. They asked all of the sons of the brother of Jared to serve them as king, but none would agree. They then asked the sons of Jared; all of them refused but the last one, and he accepted. His name was Orihah. He began to reign, and the people continued to prosper until they became very rich. Orihah was humble and righteous, and he remembered his father's teachings. He taught the people to serve the Lord and keep his commandments. During his reign, both Jared and his brother died and were buried there in the Promised Land.

CHAPTER FIVE

The Jaredites' First War

Ether 7.

THE SECOND king of the Jaredites was named Kib. During his reign the first war took place among the Jaredites, and in it brother fought against brother.

This war started as a fight between a father and his son. The father was Kib, second king of the Jaredites. He had trouble with his son, Corihor, who rebelled against him and took his family into a nearby land known as Nehor. The king, Kib, lived in the land of Moron.

Corihor's sons and daughters were very handsome, and attracted some of Kib's people into the land of Nehor. As more and more people came into his land, Corihor organized them into an army. Corihor was an ambitious man, and wanted to be king. He was even willing to fight his own father and his own brothers, in order to have the throne.

After he had trained his army, Corihor marched against his father, Kib, who reigned in the land of Moron. He captured him and made him his prisoner. Then he seized the throne and began to rule over the people. He continued to reign for many years, keeping Kib, his father a prisoner. Kib was allowed to have members of his family with him in captivity. One son was born to him during this time, a boy named Shule.

When Shule grew up and learned that his older brother was keeping their father a prisoner, having taken his throne from him, he became angry. Shule was a strong man, and very wise.

Going to a hill called Ephraim, Shule began to dig metal from a mine. This he made into swords of steel. He talked with his friends and the friends of his father, and with them planned to take the kingdom away from Corihor and give it back to Kib.

12

They armed themselves with the swords Shule had made in the mountain of Ephraim, and marched back to Nehor where they fought with Corihor and his army. They defeated Corihor, rescued Kib, the true king, and restored him to the throne.

Kib was a very old man at this time, and because Shule had restored the kingdom, Kib chose him to be king in his place. Shule, being a wise man, lived righteously, and ruled the people well. Under his direction they grew in numbers, and prospered in the land.

When Corihor saw how wisely Shule reigned, he repented of his wickedness, and Shule then gave him some authority in the kingdom. But Corihor had a son named Noah, who was evil, and desired the kingdom for himself. Noah organized an army and rebelled against Shule. Corihor was loyal to Shule, and helped to fight his own son in the rebellion. Noah captured a part of the land and set himself up as king over that. Later he gained more strength, and started another war against Shule. This time he captured Shule and planned to put him to death. But one night the sons of Shule entered Noah's house and killed him. Then they broke down the doors of the prison, rescued their father, and gave him back his throne.

Cohor, one of the sons of Noah, would not serve under Shule. He took as many people as would follow him, and set up another kingdom. This divided the people so that there were now two kingdoms among the Jaredites, the Kingdom of Shule, and the Kingdom of Cohor.

Cohor had a son named Nimrod. When Nimrod became king over his father's kingdom, he surrendered to Shule, so the two kingdoms were reunited.

During these wars the people became so wicked that the Lord sent prophets among them to warn them of their sins. When the prophets called them to repent, the people mocked them and persecuted them. But Shule punished those who reviled the proph-

13

ets, and passed a law to protect them and permit them to preach any time and in any way they desired.

As the prophets continued to preach, and King Shule protected them, the people began to listen to them, and repented of their sins. They stopped fighting among themselves. In this way peace was restored to the land, and there were no more wars as long as King Shule lived.

In their wickedness the people had apostatized from the true gospel, and had begun to worship before images, which was a great sin in the eyes of the Lord. Now that they began to repent, they put away their idols, and worshipped the true God once more.

Shule remembered the story of his fathers, and how they had been brought across the great waters to the Promised Land, and he remembered the promises the Lord had made to them. Humbly he ruled in righteousness the rest of his life.

CHAPTER SIX

A Wicked Princess

Ether 8 and 9.

KING OMER was an upright ruler of the Jaredites, but he had a wicked son named Jared who plotted to be king instead of his father. Jared spoke flattering words to the people and many of them followed him. At last, by his cunning talk, he gained half of the kingdom. Then with his army he began a war against his father. Following the wicked example of Corihor, Jared captured Omer and carried him away. Then he set himself up as king over all the kingdom.

Omer lived half his life in captivity, and some of his children were born to him then. Among them were two sons who were angry at their wicked brother Jared for holding their father prisoner. So they gathered their friends around them, and one night attacked the army of Jared and killed them all. They were about to kill Jared also, but he pleaded so for his life, that they felt sorry for him and let him live.

But Jared did not repent. Again he made plans to become king. Jared had a beautiful daughter, who was as wicked as he was. Seeing her father's displeasure because he was no longer king, she offered to help him regain the throne.

She told him of a powerful but wicked man named Akish. She planned to dance before him and please him so that he would wish to marry her. When he would ask Jared for consent to the marriage she told him to say, "I will give her if ye will bring unto me the head of my father, the king."

Jared sent for Akish and did as his evil daughter had told him. The princess danced before Akish, and pleased him so much that he asked for her hand in marriage. The wicked Jared then

15

JARED'S DAUGHTER DANCES BEFORE AKISH.

said, "I will give her unto you if you will bring unto me the head of my father the king."

Akish was so anxious to have the beautiful dancer for his wife that he was willing to kill the king to get her. But he knew he must have help, so he gathered together all his friends and relatives and told them he wanted to form a secret order with them as members. Akish said that each one must take an oath to do whatever he asked them to do. These men took the oath and joined. They also took an oath that they would kill any of their own members who told what happened in their meeting or what their promises were.

After putting them all under oath, Akish told them that they must help him kill the king and again give Jared the throne. They all promised to help.

The Lord loved the righteous King Omer, and when Akish and his wicked helpers made their plot to kill him, the Lord

16

warned Omer and told him to flee from the land. Taking all
his family except Jared, who sought his life, Omer left his home
and traveled many days into the wilderness. At last he came
to a place by the sea known as Ablom, and there he made his
new home.

When Jared learned that his father had left the kingdom,
he took the throne for himself, and began once more to rule as
king. He gave his wicked daughter in marriage to Akish, though
Akish had not killed Omer.

But Akish himself now wanted to be king. He went to his
followers who had joined his secret group, and asked them to kill
Jared so that he himself could get the throne.

One day as Jared sat listening to the needs of his people,
the oath-bound followers of the wicked Akish killed him, and
Akish became king.

One of the sons of Akish was a popular young man named
Nimrah. Akish became jealous of Nimrah, and had him shut up
in prison without food or water until he died.

Nimrah had several brothers. One of them became so angry
at what Akish had done to Nimrah that he left the kingdom
and went to live with the good king Omer. The other sons of
Akish had joined their father's secret order, and had taken the
evil oaths. Becoming angry with their father, they began to offer
money to the people if they would follow them. The people of
Akish were as greedy for money as Akish was for power, and
many of them followed the sons of Akish as long as they gave
them money. It was not long until a large army followed these
sons, who then began a war against their father. The fighting
went on for several years, and the destruction was so great that
by the time their last battle was fought there were only thirty
people left alive in the entire kingdom. These left the battlefields
and went to live with King Omer.

Inasmuch as all of Omer's enemies had been killed, he once
more began to rule over the whole land.

CHAPTER SEVEN

The Poisonous Snakes

Ether 9.

*T*HE PROMISED Land as you know, is divided into two con-
tinents, which are joined by a narrow neck of land.

The descendants of Jared and his brother who came from
the Tower in the Old World, lived in the land northward, as
they spoke of it; north of the "narrow neck of land."

One of the good kings of the Jaredites was named Emer.
He was so faithful to the Lord that the Savior appeared to him.
He lived in peace all his life, and the people over whom he
reigned were also righteous during his lifetime. For this reason
the Lord blessed and prospered them.

The people became very numerous again and spread out
over the land. Years after the death of the good king Emer, there
arose a king among the people named Heth. He was a wicked
man, and organized again the secret order which Akish had
started among the people of his day. Heth put its members
under oath to follow him in committing crimes against the people,
to get gain for themselves, as they thought.

Always it has seemed that when a righteous king ruled over
the people, he persuaded them to be good, but when a wicked king
ruled, he taught them wicked practices. This was the case with
King Heth. He had killed his father, the former king, in order
to have the throne for himself. And he taught his people wickedness, so that they too became evil. This angered the Lord, who
sent his prophets among them, warning them that they would
be destroyed unless they would repent. The prophets said that
God would send a curse upon the land, and there would be a
famine, so that many people would die of starvation.

But the people would not believe the prophets. The king

18

was so angry with them that he commanded the people to kill them or drive them out. They forced many of them to leave the kingdom; others they arrested, and put in deep pits in the ground where they were left to die.

Because his prophets were rejected, the Lord now sent the curse upon the land. No rain fell, the crops dried up, and the people began to starve. Still they would not repent.

Then the Lord sent a plague of poisonous serpents. Many people were bitten by these snakes. So were the cattle, and they became so frightened of the snakes that they began to run southward away from them.

As the flocks ran, many of them died by the way. The people followed their flocks, and as the animals died, the starving people ate them. Many of the animals escaped into the "land southward" as the country south of the "narrow neck of land" was known in those days.

When the people tried to follow them they found the way closed up so that they could not pass because the Lord had caused large numbers of serpents to gather there. All who tried to get through were bitten by the snakes and died.

Faced now with death, either from snake-bite or from the famine in the northland, the people remembered what the prophets had told them, and they began to repent. They prayed to the Lord for relief and humbled themselves so that the Lord sent rains upon the earth. The crops began to grow once more, and the people were able to get food.

But many people had died of starvation. Among them were the wicked King Heth and all his family except one son, whose name was Shez. Having learned the lesson the Lord had taught the people, Shez lived a righteous life. He tried to repair the damage done during the lifetime of his wicked father, and he taught his people to serve God, who had saved them from the famine.

CHAPTER EIGHT

The Jaredites Destroyed

Ether 9 to 15.

*W*HEN THE people who suffered in the famine and plague of snakes began to repent and serve the Lord, they also began to prosper.

One thing they greatly desired was to destroy the serpents which blocked their road into the land southward. They wanted to go into the south land, and hunt for game. When at last they were able to kill the serpents, many people went into the south land where they found animals in great numbers. They decided that they would build no cities in that part of America, but would keep it for hunting.

Many years went by, and the people became so numerous that they numbered into the millions. As they became strong, they also became wicked. Prophets came among them, and warned them that they would be destroyed if they did not repent. The Lord had said that America was a choice land, which he had kept for the righteous, and he would not permit the wicked to live here for long. The people would not believe the prophets, and rejected their teachings.

In the days of a king named Coriantumr, the prophet Ether came among the people. The Lord sent Ether to the king, with instructions to tell him that if he and his family would turn from their sins, the Lord would spare the people and allow Coriantumr to keep the throne and rule over them. But if they would not repent, all the people would be destroyed including Coriantumr's family. Coriantumr alone would remain alive, and he would be spared only to see another people possess the land. This other people would be brought to America by the Lord himself, just as the Jaredites had been.

Instead of repenting, Coriantumr's people tried to kill Ether, but the prophet escaped, and hid in a cave in the rocks.

A civil war broke out among the people. A leader named Lib arose, gathered an army about him, and began to fight Coriantumr. Lib was a giant, taller than any other man in the kingdom. As the armies attacked, Lib and Coriantumr fought together, and Coriantumr was wounded. Later in the battle Lib was killed, and his brother Shiz took command of his troops.

Shiz heard that Ether had said Coriantumr would not be slain in battle, but he did not believe the word of the Lord. He was very angry at Coriantumr because Lib had been killed, and he determined to slay Coriantumr in revenge.

The war between the two armies became so bitter that large numbers of people lost their lives. Each army, as it went through the country, tried to force the people living there to join with them and fight. If they refused they were killed, men, women and children.

One day Coriantumr was sorely wounded and was carried off the battlefield as though he were dead. But he began to recover. While he lay there getting well, he counted up the losses in the war. He saw that there had been nearly two million soldiers killed, besides their wives and children. He began to repent of his evil ways, and remembered what Ether had told him.

He wrote a letter to Shiz, and offered to give up his throne if Shiz would stop the war. Shiz replied that if Coriantumr would give himself up to be slain, Shiz would spare the people and stop the war. Coriantumr would not give himself up, so the fighting went on. One time the armies of Shiz would be victorious; then again the armies of Coriantumr would win. The tide of battle went back and forth. The soldiers fought all day, and at night they slept on their swords, ready to begin the battle again next morning.

Coriantumr gathered his people about a hill called Ramah,

which is the same hill which was later known as Cumorah. There they fought as the armies of Shiz came against them. Day by day the battle went on, and many people lost their lives. At last there were only fifty-two left in the army of Coriantumr, and sixty-nine in the army of Shiz. Next day they fought again, and when night came, only thirty-two of the men of Shiz were left alive, and twenty-seven followers of Coriantumr.

The next day they fought, and more were killed. By the next day, only Shiz and Coriantumr were left alive. They fought until both were weak from loss of blood. Shiz fainted. Coriantumr leaned upon his sword to rest, and then he killed Shiz. Coriantumr was the only one left. He fell to earth, and lay there unconscious.

The Lord now told Ether to leave his cave. He went out and saw the destruction of the Jaredites, which was a result of their wickedness.

He wrote what he saw, and then hid the plates on which he had written his story.

When Coriantumr recovered from his wounds, and discovered that he was the only man left alive, he wandered southward.

In the meantime, the Lord had brought the Nephites to America. Coriantumr continued to wander southward until he came to the city of Zarahemla, and there he saw what Ether had also predicted — another people possessing the land. He lived with these people until he died.

CHAPTER NINE

God Chooses A New People

1 Nephi 1 and 2.

*W*HEN THE Lord told Ether that he would send another people to inherit America if the Jaredites would not repent, he had in mind a righteous family in Jerusalem. This was the family of a prophet named Lehi. Lehi's wife was named Sariah, and they had four sons, Laman and Lemuel, Nephi and Sam.

Lehi was a wealthy man, with many possessions. He served the Lord, and taught his family to do likewise. He lived in the days of the wicked King Zedekiah, about 600 years before the birth of the Savior. At this time, the Babylonians were making war upon the Jews, and threatening to carry them away into captivity.

Many prophets came among the people, telling them that if they did not repent, the Lord would permit the Babylonians to destroy their city, and carry them off into slavery. Lehi was one of these prophets.

One day while Lehi was praying to the Lord to spare the people, a pillar of fire came down from heaven and stood upon a large rock before him. As he looked, the Lord revealed to him what would happen to the people and also to the city of Jerusalem. What he was told made Lehi tremble with fear. He was so over-powered by the Spirit of the Lord that he hurried home and lay down in his bed. While there, he was shown another vision by the Lord. He saw the heavens open and the Lord sitting upon his throne, surrounded by large numbers of angels, singing and prais-ing God.

He saw descending from heaven a glorious being, surrounded by light brighter than the noon-day sun. He was followed by twelve others. They came down to the earth and approached Lehi,

23

and gave him a book. When Lehi opened it he read in it many things about Jerusalem and that it would be destroyed because of the wickedness of the people. He was also shown that soldiers would come into the city, seize the people, and carry them off as slaves into Babylon.

After he had seen these things, Lehi arose from his bed and went out once more among the people of the city. He told them of the vision and what he had seen. The Jews at first made fun of him, and then as he continued to preach they became angry. They had tried to kill other prophets who came before Lehi, and had stoned many of them. Now they tried to kill him.

The Lord loved Lehi, and warned him of their plans. He told his prophet to take his family and go into the wilderness, leaving all their possessions behind.

They were obedient to the Lord and left the city at once, leaving behind them all of their property, their gold and silver and other precious things. They took only tents in which to live, and provisions, so that they would not be hungry in the wilderness.

They traveled for three days to the shores of the Red Sea. There they pitched their tents in a valley, by the side of a river. Lehi then built an altar and made an offering to the Lord to thank him for saving their lives.

Nephi and Sam were righteous boys, and believed in the teachings of their father, but Laman and Lemuel were rebellious. They grumbled because their father had taken them into the wilderness, and longed to go back home to live in comfort in the city.

When Laman and Lemuel complained, Lehi spoke to them sharply, so that they trembled before their father, and did as he told them to do.

Nephi prayed to the Lord, desiring to know what the Lord would have them do. God spoke to this righteous boy, and told him that he and the other members of the family were to be led to a choice land — most choice above all other lands in the world, where they could become a mighty people.

The Lord also told Nephi that if he continued to be faithful, he would be a ruler over his older brothers.

Nephi told his brother Sam what the Lord had said, and Sam believed him.

Nephi tried to preach to his two older brothers, but they would not believe what he said, and grew more angry with him.

Their refusal to listen hurt Nephi's feelings, and he went to the Lord in prayer. The Lord spoke to him by revelation, and told him that he would be greatly blessed because of his faithfulness. The Lord again said that he would bring the family to the Promised Land, where Nephi and his loved ones would be prospered. But Laman and Lemuel would not be prospered there. Their sins had angered the Lord, who now said, "Behold in that day they shall rebel against me, I will curse them even with a sore curse, and they shall have no power over thy seed except they also shall rebel against me.

"And if it so be that they rebel against me, they shall be a scourge unto thy seed, to stir them up in the ways of remembrance."

CHAPTER TEN

The Plates of Brass

*T*HE Lord planned to bring Lehi and his family to the Promised Land to become a great people. But he desired that after they
arrived there, they should continue to worship him and keep his
commandments.

Many teachings of the ancient prophets were contained in
the scriptures which were kept by the Jews. It was the wish of the
Lord that Lehi take these scriptures with him on his journey so
that he and his people could read the teachings of his prophets.

In ancient times records were kept in various ways. Some
were put on clay tablets which were baked hard after the writings were placed upon the soft clay. Others were written with ink
upon papyrus which was a paper-like substance made from reeds
or rushes found in swamps. Many were engraved upon metal
plates, some of gold, others of brass.

Through a dream, the Lord told Lehi to send his sons back
to Jerusalem to get the scriptures. They were to go to the house of
Laban who was the keeper of the records. Laban had plates of
brass which contained the teachings of the prophets and the history of the Jews. They also contained family records, including
that of Lehi and his family.

Lehi told Nephi, his faithful son, of this new commandment
of the Lord, and asked him and his brothers to return to the city
for the records, and bring them to him in the wilderness. When
Lehi explained what must be done, Nephi gladly agreed to go
and said: "I know that the Lord giveth no commandments unto
the children of men save he shall prepare a way for them that
they may accomplish the thing which he commandeth them."

Lehi was greatly pleased when he heard this, and sent the

four boys on the journey. When they came near Jerusalem, the boys drew lots among themselves to decide who of them should go to the house of Laban for the records. The lot fell to Laman. He entered the city and soon found Laban. When he asked for the records, Laban became angry and accused the young man of being a robber. Laman turned quickly and ran to his brothers outside the city walls.

The two older boys were discouraged and wished to return to their father in the wilderness without the records. But Nephi knew that the Lord had sent them, not alone their father. He thought of the many riches they had left behind when they first left the city, and believed that if they were offered to Laban, he might give them the records in exchange. His brothers thought this a good plan, and agreed to try it.

They all went to their home in Jerusalem, gathered together all of their father's valuables, and took them to Laban, offering to give them to him, if in return he would give them the brass plates. Laban was a greedy man, and when he saw the precious things he desired to have them. He called his servants and ordered them to kill the four brothers, so that these riches might be his.

When Laban's servants drew their swords to kill them, the young men ran for their lives, not stopping until they were outside of the city walls. Fearing they would be followed, they hid in a cave, and talked over their trouble. What would be their next move?

The older brothers were discouraged and became angry when Nephi asked them to try again. They struck him with a rod and as they did so, an angel of the Lord appeared, and rebuked them. The angel told them all to return to Jerusalem, and promised that this time the Lord would deliver Laban into their hands.

After the angel had vanished, Laman and Lemuel still complained. They felt that if Laban had command over fifty men, he would have little trouble killing the four of them.

Nephi told them that the Lord was mightier than Laban and his fifty, or even ten thousand, and that he could protect them and help them to get the records. At last his brothers agreed to return, but when they reached the walls of the city, the older ones re-fused to go farther. Nephi might go, if he wished, but not they.

When night came, Nephi left his brothers in hiding and crept into the city. As he neared Laban's house, he noticed a man who seemed to be drunk. This man fell to the ground in a stupor just as Nephi approached him. Coming closer, Nephi found that it was Laban himself, dressed in armor as if ready to fight, with his sword at his side.

As Nephi stood there the Spirit of the Lord told him to kill Laban, but Nephi was afraid and hesitated. The voice came again commanding him to take Laban's life, adding, "The Lord hath delivered him into thy hands. It is better that one man should perish than that a nation should dwindle and perish in unbelief."

Nephi drew the sword from the sheath and killed him. He then removed the armor and put it on himself, with the sword at his side. He hurried to Laban's house where he was greeted by Zoram, the servant in charge, who mistook him for Laban. Nephi, speaking in a voice like Laban's, told Zoram to bring the brass plates to him, which he did.

As Nephi took them, he asked Zoram to follow him. They walked swiftly to where the three brothers waited, outside the walls of the city. When Nephi, still dressed in Laban's armor, came toward them, they thought that Nephi had been killed, and that Laban and his servant were now coming after them. They started to run away but Nephi called to them, and when they recognized his voice they returned.

For the first time, realizing that Nephi was not Laban, Zoram tried to escape, but Nephi caught him and held him. He told Zoram they would spare his life if he would stay with them. Nephi did not want Zoram to return to spread the alarm. When the

28

servant agreed to go with them to Lehi's camp, they left together, and not long afterward delivered the plates to their father.

Nephi knew that he must win Zoram's confidence and friendship, for he did not wish to kill him, neither did he wish to let him return to Jerusalem. He must join Lehi's family, and travel with them.

Nephi said to Zoram, "Surely the Lord hath commanded us to do this thing, and shall we not be diligent in keeping the commandments of the Lord? Therefore, if thou wilt go down into the wilderness to my father thou shalt have place with us."

Zoram took courage from the words of Nephi, and promised to go with him. He also took an oath that he would remain with him, and never try to escape. Nephi did not worry about him after that. Zoram kept his promise, and became a member of the family, and travelled to America with them.

CHAPTER ELEVEN

Ishmael Accepts the Call

1 Nephi 7.

*L*EHI and Sariah were overjoyed when their sons came back to them. During their long absence they had been worried, and Sariah had begun to complain. She was not sure that her husband had been inspired of the Lord to leave their comfortable home and travel in the wilderness; and she wondered if he had done right to ask their sons to risk their lives in getting the records from Laban.

But when the boys reached camp, Sariah was sorry she had complained. Filled with joy at their return, she told Lehi that now she surely knew that the Lord had commanded him to lead the family into the wilderness. She knew too that the Lord had protected their sons, and had delivered them from the hands of Laban. The family again offered sacrifice to the Lord to show their gratitude for his blessings.

Lehi could hardly wait to read the plates of Laban. As soon as he had welcomed his sons back and offered sacrifice to the Lord, he began to read them. He found that they contained the writings of Moses, which told of the creation of the world and the story of Adam and Eve, our first parents. On them also were written many prophecies by the Jewish prophets. These Lehi prized greatly. He found the genealogies of his own people, and discovered that he was a descendant of Joseph who had been sold into Egypt.

Curiously enough, he found that Laban, who had been keeper of these records, was also a descendant of Joseph. So Lehi and Laban were related.

Lehi was now more than ever thankful that the Lord had helped Nephi to get the records. Filled with the Spirit of the

Lord, Lehi prophesied that the writings on the plates of brass would last forever, and would never be dimmed by time.

Again the Lord spoke to Lehi, telling him that it was not his will that he, his wife, and their sons should travel alone into the wilderness. The sons should have wives so that they could rear families of their own when they reached the Land of Promise.

There was a righteous man in Jerusalem named Ishmael, who had several daughters. If Ishmael and his family would join them, the sons of Lehi and the daughters of Ishmael could marry. So the Lord commanded that the boys should go again to Jerusalem and bring Ishmael and his family to the wilderness.

When they reached the city, they called at Ishmael's home, and told him about their journey. The Lord poured out his spirit upon Ishmael and softened his heart, so that he believed all that the young men told him, and agreed to join them, with his family.

After leaving the city, Laman and Lemuel and two of the daughters of Ishmael rebelled. They longed for the comfort of city life. They disliked the hardships of the wilderness, and were determined to return to Jerusalem.

Nephi spoke sharply to them, and told them that the journey was commanded by the Lord himself. He reminded them that they had seen an angel, and had been delivered out of the hands of Laban. The older brothers became still more angry, and seized Nephi. They tied him up with cords and threatened to kill him. Their plan was to leave him helpless in the wilderness where wild beasts would come and devour him.

Lying on the ground bound tightly, Nephi prayed to the Lord for strength. As he did so, the cords on his hands and feet were loosened, and he stood up before his astonished brothers, talking to them as before.

Laman and Lemuel tried again to hold him so that they could tie him more securely, but one of the daughters of Ishmael pleaded with the angry boys to let him alone.

31

Her mother and brother also begged the older boys to let Nephi go. At last they did so and began their journey again, reaching Lehi's camp in safety.

Laman and Lemuel became very repentant after this, and begged Nephi for forgiveness. They even bowed down before him, and pleaded with him for forgiveness for what they had done to him.

Nephi wrote of this afterward, and said, "And it came to pass that I did frankly forgive them all that they had done, and I did exhort them that they would pray unto the Lord their God for forgiveness. And it came to pass that they did so."

When they had arrived in Lehi's camp, they all rejoiced together for their safe arrival, and offered burnt offerings to the Lord for his blessings.

Although Laman and Lemuel were so humble at this time, their repentance did not last long, and they soon began to rebel once more against both Nephi and their father Lehi.

CHAPTER TWELVE

Nephi's Vision

1 Nephi 9-15.

*T*HE LORD commanded Nephi to keep a record of his people. It was to be made so that it would last for centuries. So Nephi made very thin plates of gold, which formed a book when bound together. Upon these plates he engraved his record.

One of the wonderful things Nephi wrote was a great vision which was given to him of the Lord. He was shown the land of Palestine as it would be at the time of the birth of the Savior, and the beautiful virgin, Mary, who was to become his mother. Later he saw Mary, this time with the child Jesus in her arms.

The next part of the vision showed John the Baptist, who was sent to prepare the way before the Savior. He saw that John baptized Jesus, and after the baptism, the Holy Ghost came down out of heaven in the sign of a dove. He was shown that Jesus chose twelve apostles, who went with him throughout the land preaching the gospel, healing the sick, and casting out evil spirits.

Then he saw that Jesus was raised up on a cross, and that he died for the sins of all mankind. After Jesus had been put to death, the vision revealed that the people of the world fought against the apostles of the Lord.

Nephi's vision continued showing the land of promise to which Lehi was leading them. It made known that Laman and Lemuel and their wives would break away from Nephi, Sam and their families, and become a separate nation. Because of their wickedness they would be cursed with a dark skin, and be known as Lamanites.

In this vision was shown also the future history of the Nephites (as the descendants of Nephi and Sam were to be called). He saw that the two nations fought, and that many lives were lost in these wars. It was made known also that after his resurrection in Palestine, the Savior would come among the Nephites; that both the Nephites and the Lamanites would be converted to his teachings, and that they all would become one happy, peaceful nation. This time of peace was to last for two hundred years.

After this some of the people would become wicked. They would take upon themselves the name of Lamanites and their skins once more would become dark. At last Nephi saw the Lamanites destroy the Nephites. Then they became a dark and filthy people, full of idleness and sin.

Next the vision showed the nations of Europe and a man there upon whom the Spirit of God descended. Inspired by it he sailed over the seas and came to the Land of Promise and for the first time saw the Lamanites, whom he called Indians. This man was Columbus who discovered America.

Other people followed him to the Land of Promise, and established a great nation in what became known as America. These colonists made war against their mother-country. The Lord blessed them and helped them win their freedom from the "mother gentiles." The colonists spread out over the land, forcing the Indians to flee before them. The Indians, or Lamanites, were not able to defend themselves, and finally became a helpless people.

The Lord showed Nephi the history of the whole world even to the end, but would not allow him to write all of it. He told the young prophet that another of the Lord's servants, one of the apostles, would write the other part. This man was John, the beloved disciple of Jesus, sometimes called the Revelator.

Nephi told his brothers about the vision, and urged them to keep the commandments so that they would not rebel and suffer the curse which he had seen come upon them in the vision. The brothers listened attentively to what Nephi said, and believed him. They were humbled, and said they wished to serve the Lord. This made Nephi very happy.

Each of the sons of Lehi married a daughter of Ishmael, and Zoram, who stayed with them, married the oldest daughter of the family.

After the marriages, the Lord spoke again to Lehi and told him the time had come to begin once more the long journey to the Promised Land. The next morning Lehi found outside of his tent a round ball made of brass. Within the ball were two spindles which acted like a compass in pointing the way they should take on their journey.

They gathered together their provisions, took down their tents, and began their trip. As they travelled they had to obtain more food, so the young men made bows and arrows and hunted game in the wilderness.

CHAPTER THIRTEEN

They Build a Ship

1 Nephi 17-18.

*T*HE little brass ball or director pointed the way for the travellers as they walked farther and farther into the wilderness. They called it the Liahona. They lived on wild berries and fruit which they found along the way, and game which they killed with their bows and arrows. The Lord inspired them not to use fires, so they had to eat all of their food raw, including the meat. But the Lord made their food sweet to their taste, and blessed them so that they were healthy and strong.

After a long journey they reached the shores of a beautiful sea, which they called "Many Waters," because it was so great. Wild fruit trees grew along the shore, and so abundant was the food that Lehi and his company called the place "Bountiful." There were mountains nearby, making it a scene of great beauty. They made a camp in Bountiful, and decided to rest there for a time.

One day the voice of the Lord came to Nephi saying, "Arise, get thee into the mountain." Nephi climbed the large mountain nearby and there asked the Lord what he desired. The Lord answered and said, "Thou shalt construct a ship after the manner which I shall show thee, that I may carry thy people across these waters." He also told Nephi that he would help him, which comforted him greatly. But Nephi knew that he would need tools. He remembered that ore could be mined from the mountains, and that if he could find it, he could smelt it and get metal to make tools.

Nephi was told by the Lord where to find ore. He then took the skins from wild beasts which he killed, and made a bellows to blow his fire.

Nephi bound by his brothers . .

He gathered twigs and bark of trees, and set fire to them by striking two stones together. Putting more fuel upon the flames, he soon had a hot fire burning. It became hotter as he used his bellows, and he began to melt the ore from which he made tools to build the ship.

This was a big undertaking, and Nephi needed help. To build a ship large enough to carry so many people and so much food across the ocean would require much work. He went back to camp and asked his brothers to help him. When they heard of his plan, they laughed at him, and told him he did not know how to build a ship. They tried once more to hurt him. Filled with the spirit of the Lord he cried out to his brothers saying that if they so much as touched him, they would wither and die. The older brothers were frightened.

The Lord told Nephi that he would shock Laman and Lemuel to show them that the Spirit of the Lord was with him. He told Nephi to stretch out his hand. As his arm went forward his brothers were shocked by a power they had never felt before. This was a sign to them that the Lord was with Nephi. They asked his forgiveness, and promised to help with the work.

In the forests, with their newly made tools they cut down trees and from them they began to make a boat. From time to time the Lord gave them instructions.

At last the ship was finished. Even Nephi's unhappy brothers admitted that it was well made. They felt humbled in their spirits and were thankful for the Lord's help.

The Lord now spoke to Lehi, and told him to ask the family to prepare fruits, meat, honey and other food, load it on board the ship, and make ready to sail over the ocean. They had brought with them different kinds of seeds, so that they could plant crops when they arrived in their new home.

All of the people boarded the ship, and then put out to sea.

The Lord caused winds to blow them in the direction in which they were to go.

After the ship had travelled on the ocean many days, Laman, Lemuel, and the sons of Ishmael and their wives decided to have a party. They sang and danced, and spoke very rudely. For a while they forgot that it was through the Lord's blessings that they were sailing so safely on the sea.

When he saw the sinfulness of their actions, Nephi was afraid that the Lord would be offended, and might withhold his blessings from them. He feared that without the Lord's protection, they might lose their lives in a storm. He asked them to stop their sinful behavior. Again this made his older brothers angry. They took hold of him, abused him cruelly and tied him so fast that he could not move.

At once the compass which the Lord had sent to guide them on their journey, stopped working. No one knew which way to steer the ship. A bad storm arose, and for three days and nights the ship rolled and tossed dangerously. They were helpless.

Lehi and Sariah, and Nephi's wife begged Laman and Lemuel to set him free, but instead they threatened them also. This was heart-breaking to Lehi and Sariah, but their grief had no effect on the wicked young men. The storm became worse, and on the fourth day it was so bad that it seemed the ship would sink at any moment.

At last Laman and Lemuel began to fear for their own lives. They were afraid to die. They thought that the storm must be the judgment of God because they had been so cruel to their parents and their younger brother.

The wicked but cowardly boys now returned to Nephi, and cut the ropes which held him. His wrists and ankles had become swollen, and were very sore. It was a great relief when the ropes were removed.

As soon as he was free, Nephi hurried to where he kept the

compass. As he held it, again it began to work. He then prayed to the Lord that the storm which had tossed them about for so long might be stopped. His prayer was answered and the Lord caused the sea to become calm. All on board were thankful that the storm was over. Light winds now came to carry the ship on its journey. Nephi steered the vessel on the way indicated by the compass. After many more days of travel, they reached the Promised Land, which is America.

The journey had been hard on the aged Lehi and his wife, Sariah. The quarrel which was started by Laman and Lemuel while they were still at sea, had so disturbed them that they became ill.

In writing of it Nephi said, "My parents, being stricken in years and having suffered much grief because of their children, they were brought down, yea, even upon their sick-bed.

"Because of their grief and much sorrow, and the iniquity of my brethren, they were brought near even to be carried out of this time to meet their God; yea, their grey hairs were about to be brought down to lie low in the dust; yea, even they were near to be cast with sorrow into a watery grave."

But when Nephi was released, and they all went safely ashore, they revived, and lived for some time after this.

CHAPTER FOURTEEN

New Homes in America

II Nephi 1-4.

*A*s soon as the ship reached America, the travellers went ashore. They pitched their tents which they had brought with them, and began to explore the country round about. They found there nearly everything they would need to make comfortable homes.

As they went into the forests they found animals of many kinds, including cows, horses and goats. They also found different kinds of ore, including gold and silver.

They cut timber and built houses. They plowed fields, and planted the seed which they had brought with them from the land of Jerusalem. The Lord blessed and prospered them. Their crops grew abundantly, and they began to spread out in the land.

One day the Lord gave Lehi a vision in which he revealed that the city of Jerusalem, from which they had fled, had now been destroyed by the enemies of the Jews, and that the people had been taken captive, just as Lehi had prophesied. Lehi told his family what the Lord had made known to him, and they were all thankful to be in the Land of Promise, and not in captivity among the Babylonians.

It is not pleasing to the Lord that anyone should be a slave to anyone else. The Lord had kept America hidden from the people in Jerusalem. It was to be a land of freedom, a place of refuge. He told Lehi that the people he would bring to America could have liberty here as long as they worshipped God, but if they became evil, they would either become captives of some other people or else they would be destroyed.

Lehi explained that liberty is one of the principles of the gospel and that the Lord gives it to everyone, so that each of us may

41

choose good from evil. He taught that we all have the right to choose, but that joy always follows righteousness, and sorrow comes from committing sin. He taught that "men are that they might have joy." It is the hope of the Lord that we will all have joy. Yet only those who serve God are really happy. There is no joy in sin, Lehi taught his people.

As Lehi spoke about America, he said that in the last days a great nation would be raised up here, and that it would be free. Other prophets have said the same, and Nephi saw it in vision.

Jesus told the Nephites at one time that it was "wisdom in the Father" to set up our great nation in the last days, and to make it free. It is seen from the *Book of Mormon* that the Lord has great blessings for Americans if they will obey him.

CHAPTER FIFTEEN

Lehi and Joseph Smith

II Nephi 3, 27, 30.

SEVERAL children were born to Lehi while the family travelled in the wilderness, one of them a boy named Joseph. As Lehi neared the end of his life, he called his sons to him and gave them advice concerning their future lives.

Joseph was told that he and the entire family were descendants of Joseph who was sold into Egypt. Lehi told his son that the Lord had made great promises to Joseph in Egypt, and showed him visions of things which would happen in the latter days.

Lehi said that Joseph of Egypt taught this: "Thus saith the Lord unto me: a choice seer will I raise up out of the fruit of thy loins. And unto him will I give commandments, that he shall do a work for the fruit of thy loins, his brethren, which shall be of great worth unto them, even to the bringing of them to the knowledge of the covenants which I have made with thy fathers."

In telling his sons about this, Lehi said that their descendants would write a record, which would be brought forth by a great seer of latter days. It would be used with the Bible, which was written by the Jews, to convince many people of the truthfulness of the gospel.

Lehi told his son that the great prophet of latter days would be named Joseph also and that his father too would be called Joseph.

The prophet whom Lehi spoke of was Joseph Smith, the founder of the Church of Jesus Christ of Latter-day Saints. His father was Joseph Smith, Senior, who was the first patriarch of the Church.

Lehi explained that the Nephites were descendants of Joseph of Egypt. The record which Nephi was writing was the record spoken of by Joseph of old when he said his people would write a book. That record is the *Book of Mormon.*

Nephi later prophesied about the coming forth of this book in the last days. He said it would be given to this great seer, who would translate it by the power of God.

Nephi also said that three other men would be chosen to see the plates in the last days and that they should be called "three witnesses," to bear testimony to the truthfulness of the book.

When Joseph Smith was translating the plates, the Lord told him to choose these three witnesses, and he did so. Their names were Martin Harris, David Whitmer and Oliver Cowdery. They were shown the gold plates and they also saw the angel who gave them to Joseph Smith.

Nephi said that in the latter days the *Book of Mormon* would be given to the world as a new book of scripture. He said that when it was published in the last days it would be taken, not only to the white people, but also to the Indians, who are descendants of Lehi. He said that the Indians would believe the words of the book, and that after they believed, "the scales of darkness shall fall from their eyes, and many generations shall not pass away among them, save they shall be a white and a delightsome people."

Lehi was growing old, and knew that he would not live much longer. One day he called his family together and blessed them, and also blessed the family of Ishmael. Shortly afterward, Lehi became ill and died.

Amid deep mourning, the family prepared him for burial, and laid him to rest in his new homeland. Lehi was happy before his death, because the Lord had saved them all from danger in Jerusalem, and had brought them safely to America, the land choice above all other lands.

CHAPTER SIXTEEN

Nephites and Lamanites

II Nephi 5.

*T*HE DEATH of Lehi was peaceful, but with it began a thousand years of trouble and war among his people. Laman and Lemuel and the sons of Ishmael were willing to accept Lehi as their leader during his life, but now he was gone. Nephi was the one chosen of the Lord, but Laman and Lemuel were jealous of their younger brother and would not accept his guidance.

When Nephi tried to persuade them to do right, they always became angry. They said, "Our younger brother thinks to rule over us, and we have had much trial because of him. Let us slay him that we may not be afflicted more with his words. We will not have him to be our ruler, for it belongs unto us, who are the elder brethren, to rule over this people."

Laman and Lemuel then laid plans to kill Nephi. They were murderers at heart, and the Spirit of the Lord was not with them.

While these wicked men were plotting the crime, the Lord warned Nephi, and told him to take all who would follow him, and escape into the wilderness.

Two younger boys who had been born to Lehi and Sariah during their journey were true to him, as was Sam, next to the youngest in the family at the time they left Jerusalem. Zoram, who had been the servant of Laban, was a righteous man, and he with his family joined Nephi's group. Nephi could also depend on the loyalty of his own sisters, who had been born since the family left Jerusalem. When they learned of the disagreement, they chose to go with Nephi. All who followed him were believers in the Lord.

They packed their tents and other belongings, including the ball or compass, which had guided them over the ocean,

NEPHI AND HIS FOLLOWERS ARRIVE IN THE NEW LAND OF NEPHI.

the plates of brass they had obtained from Laban, and the plates on which Nephi himself was writing. Nephi also carried with him the sword of Laban.

This faithful band hurried into the wilderness, and did not stop for many days. They came to a beautiful place which they named the land of Nephi, and there they made their homes. They sowed their seeds, and began to raise sheep and cattle. Because they served the Lord, he blessed them.

Nephi was sure that Laman and Lemuel would always be his enemies, and that they with their children would fight against him and his family. Their separation was the formation of the two great nations which lived in America for nearly a thousand years—the Nephites and the Lamanites. The Nephites were those who followed Nephi, and the Lamanites were the followers of Laman and Lemuel and the sons of Ishmael. The Lamanites

46

were cursed with a dark skin, but the Nephites were a white people like ourselves.

Knowing the bitterness in the hearts of the Lamanites, Nephi and his band made plans to defend themselves if the Lamanites attacked them. He had the sword of Laban for a pattern and from it he made many other swords. He also made shields and spears, bows and arrows.

Nephi taught the people to build homes and other buildings, and to work in wood, iron, copper, brass, gold and steel, because there was an abundance of ore in the land.

One of his great desires was to build a temple. He and his followers became skillful workmen, and they erected a beautiful temple. As the people prospered, they increased in numbers.

One day they came to Nephi and asked him to be their king. He did not want them to have a king. They were now living in the land of freedom, and he thought they should govern themselves. He was willing to be their leader and their teacher, but only when they insisted did he agree to become their king.

CHAPTER SEVENTEEN

The Nephites' First War

Jacob 1-7.

THE FIRST war between the Nephites and the Lamanites came shortly after Nephi and his followers escaped from their wicked brothers and went into the wilderness to make their new home.

The Lamanites became even more wicked after Nephi and his family and friends had left them. Not only were they wicked, but they became lazy and filthy too. They hunted wild game for a living, but they also tried to steal anything they could from other people. They knew that Nephi and his family and friends were hard workers, and were building farms and comfortable homes. Being robbers at heart, they thought they could come against these Nephites and steal their gold and silver, their animals and their food.

When they began the war, they fought hard, but the Nephites beat them back. Nephi had taught his people how to use their weapons, so they were able to defend themselves. Nephi himself led them in battle. He used the sword of Laban which he had carried with him from Jerusalem. The Lamanites were beaten so badly, that for a time they did not attack the Nephites again.

Nephi ruled his people wisely. He was a hard worker and taught them to work too. He also inspired them with his sermons, and taught them always to love the Lord and serve him. But Nephi was becoming an old man. About forty years had passed since he and his father's family had left Jerusalem. His health began to fail. He knew that he must soon pass away.

One of his younger brothers who had been born in the wilderness was an upright young man named Jacob. To him Nephi gave the golden plates on which was the history of the people. He told Jacob that he must now become the historian and write a record of all that took place among them. Soon after this Nephi died.

Jacob became a great prophet to the Nephites. He lived close to the Lord, who revealed his mind and will to him. Jacob was so blessed that he could speak in the name of the Lord and even the waves of the sea would obey him. He taught the people about Jesus, and told them that some day Jesus would be born as a little baby, and would become the Savior of the world. He preached many great sermons to the people. Some he wrote on the gold plates and they are now in the Book of Mormon. So righteous was Jacob that the Lord not only spoke to him, but also sent angels from heaven to visit him.

As they served the Lord, the people were blessed. But when through these blessings they became wealthy, they began to love their riches, and some forgot the Lord. They committed many sins, which angered the Lord greatly. Jacob called them to repentance. He told them that in some ways they were becoming more sinful than the Lamanites.

About this time there arose among them an evil man named Sherem who began to hold meetings with the people. He was a good speaker, and the people liked to hear him because he flattered them, but he taught them sinful ways.

Among the things which Sherem taught was that there was no such person as Jesus Christ. As soon as he began teaching these things, Jacob rebuked him. Jacob said that he knew Jesus lived, for the Lord had spoken to him, given him revelations, and had even sent angels to him.

Sherem said Jacob was leading the people astray. Some of the people believed what he said. But the Lord was with Jacob. Under inspiration, Jacob again rebuked Sherem, and showed him that his teachings were false. Jacob bore his testimony to him that Jesus lives and is the Savior of the world.

The sinful Sherem said, "Show me a sign." It is wicked to ask for a sign, so Jacob said, "What am I that I should tempt God to show unto thee a sign in the thing which thou knowest to be true. Yet thou wilt deny it because thou art of the devil. Nevertheless, not my will be done: but if God shall smite thee, let that be a sign unto thee that he has power, both in heaven and in earth; and also that Christ shall come."

Then the Lord did smite Sherem, who fell to the earth and became very ill. He was nursed by his friends for many days, but did not get well. One day he said to the people, "Gather together on the morrow, for I shall die; wherefore I desire to speak unto the people before I shall die."

The next day all the people came together, and he spoke to them. He denied the things which he had taught, and confessed that he had been wrong. He told them that he really did believe in Jesus the Christ and that he had been deceived by the power of the devil. He said, "I have committed the unpardonable sin, for I have lied unto God, for I denied the Christ. Because I have thus lied unto God, I greatly fear lest my case shall be awful; but I confess unto God." Then he died.

When the people heard him, and saw him die, they were greatly surprised. Then the power of God came upon them, so that they also fell to the earth, just as Sherem had fallen.

Jacob was happy, for he had asked the Lord to show the people that Sherem was wrong.

CHAPTER EIGHTEEN

The Land of Liberty

II Nephi 10.

*A*MERICA is a land of liberty, made so by the Lord himself. Nephi was shown in his vision that the Lord would set America free from all other nations.

When Jacob with his brother Nephi, preached the gospel to the people, he taught them more about this Land of Promise, and the freedom which should be here. This condition of freedom was to be enjoyed not only in the days of the Nephites, but also in the last days, during our life-time.

One day when Jacob was preaching to the people he said:

"This land shall be a land of liberty unto the Gentiles, and there shall be no kings upon the land who shall raise up unto the Gentiles." He spoke of the people who live in America in these last days.

Jacob also said that the Lord had made this promise: "I will fortify this land against all other nations. And he that fighteth against Zion shall perish, saith God."

The Prophet Joseph Smith said that all of America is Zion, but there will also be a city which shall be called Zion. It will be built in Jackson County, Missouri.

Then the Lord, through the Prophet Jacob added: "He that raiseth up a king against me shall perish, for I the Lord the king of heaven, will be their king, and I will be a light unto them forever, that hear my words."

Jacob continued speaking, and said:

"Wherefore, he that fighteth against Zion, both Jew and Gentile, both bond and free, both male and female, shall perish; for they who are not for me are against me, saith our God. * * *

"Wherefore, I will consecrate this land unto thy seed, and them who shall be numbered among thy seed forever, for the land of their inheritance; for it is a choice land, saith God, unto me, above all other lands, wherefore I will have all men that dwell thereon that they shall worship me, saith God."

Jesus is the God of this Land of Promise. Therefore he commands that all who live in America shall serve him.

There have been attempts made to set up kings in America in these last days. One of them was in Mexico, when France set up a king. But he was killed, and no one else was chosen to take his place.

Once George Washington was asked to be king, after he had defeated the British armies, But he refused, and said that there should not be a king in America, for the people must have their own freedom, and should govern themselves.

Freedom is a gift of God. He intends that all men should have their liberty to choose their own course of action.

CHAPTER NINETEEN

The Prayer of Enos

Book of Enos.

*T*HE LAMANITES became worse as time went on and planned more wars against the Nephites. The Nephites sent missionaries among them to try to convert them in the hope of obtaining peace. But the Lamanites were ferocious and blood-thirsty.

They lived on beasts which they killed in the forests. They did not build homes for themselves but lived in tents, moving from place to place as they hunted for game.

They were filthy in their habits and did not wear clothes as they did in the days of Lehi, but only a short girdle about their hips. They shaved their heads as some Indians do today and lived like savages.

They made many bows and arrows and little axes which they used in battle. Although they sometimes fought among themselves, their great desire was to fight against the Nephites.

The Nephites built homes, made farms, and grew many kinds of grain and other foods. They also had herds of cows, flocks of sheep and goats, and many horses.

Prophets came among the Nephites in those days, preaching repentance, for they too had become a wicked people. One of them was Enos, the son of Jacob. Enos knew that the Lord would destroy the Nephites if they continued to live in sin.

One morning he went into the forest alone. He had a great desire to draw near to the Lord, and ask for forgiveness of his own sins. He knelt down in the woods and began to pray. He felt that he should receive an answer before he arose from his knees. He prayed all morning and afternoon, and when night came he was still praying. Then he heard the voice of God speaking to him and saying, "Enos, thy sins are forgiven thee and thou shalt be blessed."

Enos was overjoyed with this message. But he had more to ask of the Lord. He was happy for the forgiveness of his own sins, but he was troubled because of the sins of the people. He also feared for the safety of the gold plates on which the record was being kept, for the Lamanites had said they not only would kill the Nephites but would destroy their records too.

Enos now prayed that the Lord would preserve the record, even though the Nephites were all slain by the Lamanites. He prayed so long and earnestly for this blessing that the Lord spoke to him again, and he said that his desire would be granted. The records would be preserved. He also told Enos that his fore-fathers had prayed for the same blessing.

CHAPTER TWENTY

Others in the Land

Book of Omni.

ONE OF THE kings of the Nephites was named Mosiah. In his day the people were so wicked that the Lord told him to gather together all those who were righteous, and move to another place.

Those who believed in God followed Mosiah into the wilderness. This was the second time the Lord had called the righteous from among the wicked since bringing the Nephites to America. Once before, when Nephi was still alive he had told him to leave his homeland, where Laman and Lemuel were leading the people into wickedness, and go to another place.

As Mosiah led his people away none of them knew where they were going. But under the direction of the Lord, Mosiah took them deeper and deeper into the wilderness.

One day, to their great surprise, they saw that they were coming to a city, of which they had never heard. When they arrived there, they found that the people were friendly, but their language was so strange that the Nephites could not understand what they said.

Mosiah was a very wise man and a great leader. Being kind to these strangers he soon won their respect and they desired that he should be their king. They were willing to unite with the Nephites, so that they could be all one people.

This pleased Mosiah. One of the first things he did was to teach the people in this new city the language which the Nephites spoke. When they could understand one another they told King Mosiah a strange but very interesting story.

They said that they also had come from the land of Jerusalem. They had left there during the reign of the wicked king

Zedekiah, who ruled over the Jews when the Babylonians took them captive. They told Mosiah, that their leader was named Zarahemla. The Lord guided them to America, where they built this city which they called after their leader.

The reason their language was different from that of the Nephites was that they did not bring with them any of the records of the Jews. They had been in America over 200 years. As time went on, they made new words to fit their new conditions and in this way the whole language changed. The Nephites had records to help them remember how to speak the language of their fathers but their new friends had no such guide.

When the people of Zarahemla heard that the Nephites had the plates of brass they were very happy, for now they could read the scriptures, and learn about their forefathers.

One day they brought to King Mosiah a large stone with writings upon it. Inspired of the Lord, the king interpreted these inscriptions. They told about the Jaredites who had come to America from the Tower of Babel, so long before. These people were finally all killed in battle but one man, named Coriantumr who wandered southward from the region north of the narrow strip of land, and in his wanderings had come to the city of Zarahemla. There he lived for "nine moons," and then died.

It will be remembered that the Lord had told Coriantumr through the Prophet Ether, that he would live to see all his people destroyed and another people take their place in the land of America. His coming to the city of Zarahemla was a fulfilment of this prophecy.

CHAPTER TWENTY-ONE

Righteous King Benjamin

Omni 1; Words of Mormon.

WHEN MOSIAH died, his righteous son Benjamin became king of the city of Zarahemla. He loved the Lord, and served him all his days. But while he ruled the city, the Lamanites attacked his people.

King Benjamin was the keeper of the sacred records and also the sword of Laban. When the Lamanites sent their armies against Zarahemla, King Benjamin led his own fighting men against them. He used the sword of Laban in these battles, just as Nephi did when he was king.

So righteous was Benjamin, that when he called upon the Lord for help in defending his people, the Lord blessed him and his armies, and strengthened them.

With this help from God, the Nephites fought against the Lamanites with such power that they killed many thousands of them, and drove the others entirely out of their part of the country.

When peace came to Zarahemla, after this great battle, many of the people became proud, and would not serve the Lord. Others loved wickedness so much that they left Zarahemla, and went to live with the Lamanites.

Then false prophets arose among the people, and some of them even claimed to be Jesus, the Savior.

Benjamin had these men punished. But other false prophets and evil teachers began to lead the people astray.

Obtaining the help of the true prophets of the Lord, Benjamin and these righteous men preached to the people, calling them to repentance. Many were hard-hearted and would not listen, and some of these joined the Lamanites.

Benjamin and the prophets spoke with much sharpness to the people, and with the help of the Lord brought them to repentance, and then peace came to the land.

Benjamin was a righteous king, and was spoken of in those days as a "holy man." There were other "holy men" living there too, and they preached the gospel to the people with great power, and Benjamin helped them "by laboring with all the might of his body and the faculty of his whole soul."

So powerful were Benjamin and the prophets who assisted him, that they were able to stop the quarreling and fighting among the people for the remainder of the life of this king.

CHAPTER TWENTY-TWO

Benjamin's Advice

Mosiah 1-6.

*K*ING BENJAMIN had three sons, Mosiah, Helorum and Helaman. He taught them the prophecies of the Lord, and showed them how to read the ancient records which were in his possession. He explained that the records must be preserved and that the history of the people must be written on them each year.

He told them that if Lehi had not brought the plates of brass with him into the wilderness, his people would have fallen into unbelief, and become ignorant of the true God. He said Lehi could not remember all that was written on the plates, nor could the people remember all the things he taught.

Benjamin also taught his sons to believe in Jesus, who would come as the Savior of the world.

One day he called Mosiah to him, and said that he was growing old, and desired him to rule in his place. He asked Mosiah to go into all parts of the kingdom, and tell the people to meet together at the temple, so that he could speak to them.

Mosiah did as his father asked him. The people soon began to gather from all parts of the land of Zarahemla. They brought their tents and also some of their flocks to offer as sacrifices to the Lord. They had increased in number and had been prospered by the Lord under the righteous rule of Benjamin. So many gathered about the temple that Mosiah did not try to count them.

As the people assembled the crowd became so large that the temple could not hold all of them. Seeing this, Benjamin had a high tower built from which he could speak to the people. He knew that even then, all could not hear him, so he told his servants to write what he would say, and carry it to those who could not hear his voice.

59

When the people pitched their tents, the doors faced the temple, so that they could sit inside the tents and hear the king's message.

At last all was ready. The king, who now was an old man, climbed to the top of the tower and began to speak to the people. He told them that he had tried to be a good king; he had not placed heavy taxes upon them, and had even earned his own living. He told them that their real king was the Lord, who had created them, and who blessed them when they lived the way they should. He promised that if they continued to be a good people, the Lord would protect and prosper them.

Then he announced that, because he was getting too old to carry on the work of the kingdom, he had chosen his son Mosiah to be their new king.

He also said that he had been visited by an angel who told him many things, which he now desired to tell to them.

He taught them about Jesus, who soon would be born on the earth as the Savior of the world, and asked everyone to believe in him.

He spoke with such power that the people were filled with fear, because they knew that they had committed many sins. Some were so frightened because of their wrong-doing that they fell to the earth. All of them began to call upon the Lord, asking for forgiveness.

Then Benjamin spoke again. He told them that among the things they must do, if they were to please the Lord, was to love each other, to be kind to the poor and the sick, and to give to those in need.

Benjamin asked how many of the people believed what he said. They all cried with one voice, and said, "Yea, we believe all the words which thou hast spoken unto us."

They said they were willing to enter a covenant with the Lord to do his will and keep his commandments, and they did make this covenant. It pleased the aged king. He asked them to take upon themselves the name of Christ, and always serve him.

When Benjamin finished speaking, he consecrated his son to be king in his place. He gave to the young Mosiah full charge of the kingdom, all of the plates, the sword of Laban, and the ball or director, which led Lehi on his journey from the old world.

Benjamin lived for three years after this great event.

Priests were appointed to teach the people throughout the kingdom all the things which King Benjamin had told them. They went from place to place, reminding all the people of the covenant they had made at the time of Benjamin's great sermon, wherein they promised to serve God.

The new King Mosiah commanded the people to work for their living, and to till the soil and raise crops for food. He set the example by becoming a farmer himself.

CHAPTER TWENTY-THREE

Zeniff the Spy

Omni 1; Mosiah 9 and 10.

*W*HEN BENJAMIN was ruling over the city of Zarahemla, there were many who desired to return to their former home in the land of Nephi; they wished to see whether their houses were still standing, and felt that they might once more live there.

Those who wished to return gathered their friends about them and decided to make the journey. Some soldiers also joined the party. Taking with them many of their valuable possessions and much food and clothing, they armed themselves with swords and shields.

When all was ready they left the city, and started out into the wilderness. They traveled for many days, until they were near the borders of the Lamanites, and near to the land of Nephi, their former home.

Because the Lamanites were now in possession of the land, they wondered if they should attack and drive them out, or whether they should be friends with them, and enter the land in a peaceful way.

One of their number named Zeniff was well educated, and had studied the history of the Nephites. Zeniff had traveled through this country before and knew it well.

At one time, when he was a soldier in the Nephite army, he had been sent as a spy among the Lamanites, and found that there were many good people among them, and he learned to like them. He felt that the Lamanites and Nephites should be good neighbors, and live together in peace.

He told these things to the leader of the company, and to others. It made the leader angry, and he tried to kill Zeniff. But his friends came to his rescue, and saved him from death. This started a fight among the entire company. Brother fought against brother, and father fought against father. The fighting went on until nearly all of the Nephites in that group were killed. Only fifty were left alive. Zeniff was one of these. In sorrow they returned to the city of Zarahemla, and told the people of the great tragedy which had taken place.

Zeniff still wished to go back to the Lamanite country. He asked other people to join him in his plan and they agreed. He told them to bring with them their families, food and tents, and go with him into the wilderness.

After they had traveled a long time, their supplies of food gave out. Many became sick. At last they reached the place where the first company had fought among themselves.

Leaving his followers, Zeniff took four men with him and went to a nearby city of the Lamanites. There he asked to be brought before the king, whose name was Laman. Zeniff asked King Laman if he could bring his people into the land of Lehi-Nephi to make their homes.

The king was a crafty man and thought if he let them come in he might lead Zeniff and his people into a trap and make slaves of them. So he said he would turn over a part of the land to them. He ordered all the Lamanites who were living there to leave. Zeniff and his followers then moved in. They repaired the houses, and planted crops. Zeniff taught his people to serve the Lord.

After they had been there for thirteen years, King Laman decided the time had come to enslave them. He told his soldiers to start trouble with the Nephites. So the Lamanites attacked the people of Zeniff while they were in their fields, scattered their sheep, and stole much of their property. The people hurried to Zeniff for protection.

Zeniff armed them with bows and arrows, spears and shields, and organized them into an army. Then they joined in prayer to the Lord, asking him to deliver them from the hands of the Lamanites. The Lord heard their prayer, and when they met the Lamanites in battle, they defeated them; and in one day they killed more than three thousand of their enemies. Only two hundred and seventy-nine of their own brethren were killed, but for them they mourned deeply.

The Lamanites did not attack the Nephites again for a long time, but Zeniff was sure they would return. He kept his people armed with weapons of war so that they could protect themselves. He set guards in the land to watch for their enemies, but none came, and years passed in peace.

After Zeniff's people had lived there for twenty-two years, King Laman died, and his son became ruler in his place. The son was wicked, and urged the Lamanites to go to war. Zeniff had spies among the Lamanites who learned of their plans. The Nephites prepared for the battle; and when the Lamanites attacked them, they again defeated them. Once more peace came to the land.

CHAPTER TWENTY-FOUR

Lamanite False Teachings

Mosiah 10.

OFTEN wicked people tell lies to excuse their evil ways. This was true of the Lamanites. They hated the Nephites because of the many things they had which the Lamanites wanted. They were greedy, but they were too lazy to work as the Nephites did.

Not only did they hate the Nephites because of their fine homes and better crops for which the Nephites had worked hard and long, but they hated them because of their white skins. They knew that their own dark skins came as a curse from the Lord because of their evil ways. It hurt their pride to think that they were dark and the Nephites were so fair.

The Lamanites taught their children to believe many lies about the Nephites, and this increased their hate. They said that Laman and Lemuel were wronged by their father Lehi and their brother Nephi, who made them leave their pleasant home in Jerusalem and live in the wilderness. They also said that Laman and Lemuel were treated badly by Lehi and Nephi while they were traveling to America, and that while they were on the ship sailing across the ocean, Nephi abused them.

They told their children that when their forefathers first reached America, they were unfairly dealt with. They said that the Lord heard Nephi's prayers and blessed him, but would not bless Laman and Lemuel. The reason the Lord would not bless Laman and Lemuel was that they often refused to believe in the Lord, and at last rebelled and would not keep his commandments. But the Lamanites did not tell this to their children. They only taught them lies to make them hate the Nephites.

They were angry too, because Laman and Lemuel had taught them that although they were the older brothers, Nephi had taken the leadership of the family away from them. They tried to make their children and grandchildren believe that Nephi unjustly became the leader. They did not tell them that the Lord had chosen Nephi because he was willing to do what was right, and that Laman and Lemuel refused to obey him.

The Lamanites told about the time Nephi and his people fled into the wilderness to find a new home, leaving behind Laman and Lemuel and their families. The real reason they left was that Laman and Lemuel plotted to kill Nephi. The story the Lamanites told their children was that when Nephi and his family escaped into the wilderness, they robbed the Lamanites of some of their precious things. This was also false. And they said that among the most valuable of all the things which Nephi took away from them were the brass plates.

It was deceitful to teach this to their children, because Laman and Lemuel hated the teachings of the Lord which were on the plates, and would not obey them. Later the Lamanites tried to destroy the records. And yet, now they taught their children to hate the Nephites, saying that the Nephites had stolen the plates from them.

They taught them also to steal from the Nephites, and to kill them, and do all they could to destroy their homes and property. The Lamanites became more and more wild and fierce after being told so many lies by their leaders. It was because of this hatred that the Lamanites now desired to start a war against Zeniff and his people.

Zeniff's spies brought back news of their plans, and Zeniff prepared at once for war. He sent the women and children into the wilderness to hide there. Then he armed all the men with bows and arrows, spears and shields. Even the old men were placed in the army.

The spies sent out by Zeniff learned that the Lamanites were going to attack in a place called Shilom. The Nephite army went there to meet them. As the Lamanites came near, the Nephites could see that they were armed with all the weapons they knew how to make. They had bows and arrows, swords and daggers. Some had sling shots, and many carried stones to throw at the Nephites. The Lamanites had shaved their heads to make them look more fierce. Most of them were naked except for a leather cloth they wore about their hips.

Zeniff, then being an old man, led his army against the Lamanites. They had prayed for the help of the Lord, and the Lord strengthened them in their battle. They fought so well that the Lamanite army broke up and fled, leaving behind many dead and wounded.

CHAPTER TWENTY-FIVE

Wicked King Noah

Mosiah 11.

ZENIFF'S great victory over the Lamanites brought peace to his people, and they were grateful to the Lord. But now that Zeniff was old, he wished to give the kingdom to one of his sons. The boy he chose to be king was named Noah.

This young man became a wicked king. He did not serve the Lord as his father had. Not only did he live a wicked life himself, but he taught others to live the same way. When they saw how wicked the king was, they felt free to sin as he did and because of this a large part of the people became evil and forgot the Lord.

Noah made the people pay high taxes, for he wanted to live in luxury at the expense of others. He taxed them one fifth of all they had, their crops, their farm animals, their gold and silver and everything else of value.

When his father Zeniff ruled and served the Lord, he appointed good men as priests to conduct the meetings of the people. But now that Noah became king, he removed them from office. He wanted men who would not rebuke him for his sins, and who would be as proud and evil as he was himself. So he appointed men whom he called priests to have charge of the Church. This greatly displeased the Lord.

These wicked priests would not teach the true gospel to the people. Instead they taught them false doctrines, and set up images and idols and told the people to worship before them. This also made the Lord very angry, because he forbids anyone to use an image or an idol in worship.

Both the king and his evil priests made it popular to worship with idols. They said it was the right thing to do, and they flat-

68

tered the people. Many believed them, and did worship before the idols.

With all the money which he received from the heavy taxes, Noah built a beautiful palace, and many other buildings for himself and his priests and their families. They used gold and silver and other precious materials as ornaments on these buildings.

Zeniff had built a temple during his reign and the people had worshipped the Lord humbly there. But now Noah changed all this. He put costly ornaments in the temple. He made expensive seats for the priests and set up costly pulpits. These pulpits were made so that when the priests spoke to the people they did not have to stand up to speak but could recline upon them while they gave their sermons.

The king's heart was set upon riches, and getting more wealth. He planted many vineyards, and from the grapes he made much wine. He became a drunkard, and many of his people followed his example.

Noah built a high tower near the temple, and placed guards on the top to watch for the Lamanites, should any of them attack. Guards were also placed outside of the city. But there were not enough, for one day the Lamanites came and killed the guards and drove away many of their flocks and herds.

Then Noah called out his army, and attacked the Lamanites, and beat them in battle. His victorious soldiers came back, boasting of what they had done. They took pleasure in killing people and shedding their blood. This they did because of the teachings of wicked King Noah. In their boasting they said that fifty of them could stand against thousands of Lamanites. Noah had taught them to be proud as well as to tell lies.

They were now so wicked that the Lord threatened to destroy them or allow their enemies to make slaves of them.

CHAPTER TWENTY-SIX

Abinidi The Prophet

Mosiah 11-17.

*T*HE LORD always warns his people before he brings destruction upon them because of their wickedness. Sometimes though most of the people are led into sinful ways by a wicked ruler, there are some righteous among them, whom the Lord desires to save.

This was true in Noah's kingdom. To warn the wicked, and to save the righteous he sent a prophet among them. His name was Abinidi. He told the people that they would be delivered into the hands of their enemies, the Lamanites, unless they repented of their sins. The people refused to listen to him. Because their army had defeated the Lamanites but a short time before, they felt very proud and self-confident.

Abinidi continued to speak to them. "Unless this people repent and turn unto the Lord," he said, "they shall be brought into bondage."

The people became very angry with Abinidi and tried to kill him, but the Lord protected him. When King Noah heard what he was preaching, he ordered his guards to bring Abinidi to him, so that the king himself could take his life. The prophet knew of Noah's plan and hid from him.

After two years had passed, the Lord sent Abinidi out again. This time the prophet disguised himself. He preached to the people boldly and told them that unless they repented of their sins, their enemies would come upon them, kill many of them, and enslave the rest. He prophesied that hail-storms would destroy their crops and that insects would devour their grain.

Again the people were angered by what he said. This time they caught and bound him, and took him to the king. Noah

Abinidi burned at the stake . .

put Abinidi in prison and called his priests together to discuss what should be done with him.

The priests asked the king to bring Abinidi before them so that they could question him, thinking that they might trick him into making an answer that would be against their law. Then they would put him to death. But when they questioned the prophet, he spoke with such wisdom that the priests of Noah were confounded.

Abinidi rebuked the priests and preached to them from the teachings of Moses. When the king heard this, he said, "Away with this fellow and slay him."

The priests tried to take hold of Abinidi, but he cried out: "Touch me not, for God shall smite you if ye lay hands upon me, for I have not delivered the message which the Lord sent me to deliver; therefore God will not suffer that I shall be destroyed at this time."

This frightened the priests of Noah so that they did not touch him. The spirit of the Lord came upon him and his face shone with a great light, just as the face of Moses shone when he came down from the mount after talking with the Lord.

When he spoke again the king and his people listened and became afraid. Abinidi knew that King Noah and his people worshipped before idols, and he commanded them to stop it.

"Thou shalt not make unto thee any graven image, nor any likeness of things which are in heaven above or in the earth beneath. Thou shalt not bow down thyself unto them, nor serve them," he declared.

The use of images in worship has always been a crime in the sight of God, as Abinidi reminded the king and his priests. He told them also that they must not take the name of the Lord in vain, nor break the Sabbath day. They must honor their fathers and their mothers, and must not lie, steal, covet nor kill.

Turning to the king and his priests, he asked, "Have ye taught these people to keep all of these commandments? No. For if ye had, the Lord would not have sent me to prophesy evil concerning you."

Abinidi then spoke of the coming of the Savior, and prophesied that his name would be Jesus Christ; that he would perform many miracles among the people, and finally die, but that he would be resurrected.

He explained that if the people would believe the gospel, accept Jesus as the Christ and serve him, they could be saved from their sins. He told them of the judgment day, saying that every man would be punished for his own sins. "And now," he said, "ought ye not to repent of your sins?"

As Abinidi the prophet finished speaking, King Noah commanded his priests to kill him. They called soldiers who again put him in prison, while the priests decided his fate.

After three days they brought him before them, and said, "We have found an accusation against thee and thou art worthy of death."

Their accusation was that Abinidi had said that the son of God would be born into the world. They told him that if he would recall his words and deny what he had said, they would not put him to death. But unless he did, they would kill him.

Abinidi was not afraid. He said, "I will not recall the words which I have spoken, for they are true. I will suffer even to death, but I will not recall my words. They shall stand as a testimony against you."

By this time King Noah, a coward at heart, was very frightened. He wanted to release the prophet, thinking that by doing so he might save his own life. King Noah remembered that Abinidi had prophesied that he would die for his sins, and he was afraid of death. But the priests said, "He has reviled the king." This

73

stirred up the king's anger so that he ordered Abinidi put to death.

They bound and whipped him, then built a fire about him. As the flames began to scorch him he cried out, "As ye have done unto me, so ye shall be taken by your enemies and then shall ye suffer as I suffer the pains of death by fire."

As he prayed to God, saying, "Receive my soul," he died and fell into the fire.

Like many of the other prophets of the Lord, Abinidi sealed his testimony with his blood. He was loyal to the Lord to the last, and died in flames rather than deny the commandments which the Lord had given him.

In his final words, he told the wicked people there that they would be afflicted with all kinds of diseases because of their sin, and that they would be smitten on every hand, and would be driven and scattered, "even as a wild flock is driven by wild and ferocious beasts."

CHAPTER TWENTY-SEVEN

Alma Is Converted

Mosiah 18, 23-24.

ONE of the priests of King Noah believed what the martyred prophet had said. His name was Alma. When the king sought to kill Abinidi, Alma pleaded for his life. This made the king angry and he commanded his soldiers to kill Alma also. But the faithful young priest fled and went into hiding.

While the words of Abinidi were still fresh in his mind, Alma wrote all he had heard the prophet say. Then he went secretly among the people telling them about Abinidi. Many of them believed his message.

Not far from the city was a secluded spot called Mormon. Knowing that he would be killed if the king learned of his preaching, Alma took his followers there to hold meetings. Each time they met, a few more people joined them. Soon there were more than two hundred. One day Alma pointed to a beautiful fountain of water in Mormon, and began to preach baptism to his people. He told them if they truly wished to serve the Lord, they should be baptized as a sign of their devotion. He urged them to make a covenant with the Lord in baptism to serve him and keep his commandments. When he said this, the people were overjoyed.

The Lord was with Alma, and gave him the priesthood so that he could perform baptisms. The first man to be baptized was named Helam. Alma took him into the waters of Mormon and said, "Having authority from God I baptize you as a testimony that ye have entered into a covenant to serve him until you are dead." Then he immersed him in the water, and brought him up again. Others came asking for baptism, and Alma immersed each one of them. Two hundred and four persons were baptized at that time. As others in the city heard of Alma's teachings and believed, they too asked for baptism.

Those who were baptized were organized into a Church, which they called the Church of Christ. Having been given authority from the Lord, Alma now ordained priests, one for each fifty people in his fast-growing congregation. He gave them authority to preach to the people, but told them they must teach only those things which the prophets had taught.

One day the spies of the king learned of Alma's meetings, and told the wicked Noah, who sent soldiers to kill the members of the Church. Alma was warned of their coming, and took his people into the wilderness. Four hundred and fifty people followed him.

They traveled for eight days, and came to a place where there was much water and good farm land. There they made their homes. Soon a Lamanite army came near their borders, and Alma's people feared they would be killed. But Alma stood among them and encouraged them, saying that if they would be faithful their lives would be spared.

The Lord softened the hearts of the Lamanites. Alma and his followers talked with them. They discovered that the army was lost, and wished to return to the land of Nephi. The Lamanites told Alma that they would not disturb his people if he would show them the way to their own land.

But the Lamanites did not keep their promise. Being a lazy people they always wished to have other people do their work. When they saw Alma and his followers, they planned in their own minds to make slaves of them.

So instead of marching away and leaving Alma and his people in peace, the Lamanites left soldiers to guard them, while the main army went on to the land of Nephi.

The Lamanite guards were unkind to their captives. A man named Amulon also treated them badly. He was a Nephite who had left Noah's kingdom and joined the Lamanites. He knew Alma, and remembered that he had been one of King Noah's priests, and had believed the teaching of Abinidi. Amulon began to persecute Alma and his people, and make them work very hard. He put taskmasters over them who treated them very cruelly.

The people of Alma now began to cry aloud to the Lord, asking him for freedom from this slavery which had come upon them. When Amulon heard them pray, he commanded them to stop, and put guards over them to see that no one offered any more prayers. He said that if any were caught praying to the Lord, they would be killed.

Alma and his people then stopped praying aloud, but they prayed more than ever silently. The Lord knew what was in their minds, for he knows all our thoughts, and he answered their prayers.

Speaking to them, the Lord said, "Lift up your heads and be of good comfort, for I know the covenants which ye have made unto me, and I will covenant with my people, and deliver them out of bondage. And I will ease the burdens which are put upon your shoulders, that even you cannot feel them upon your backs, even while you are in bondage."

The Lord then strengthened Alma and his brethren, so that their burdens seemed light to them, and they did their work easily. They worked every day, waiting patiently for the time when the Lord would free them from the Lamanites.

So great was their faith, and so patient were they, that the Lord spoke again saying, "Be of good comfort, for on the morrow I will deliver you out of bondage."

Believing what the Lord had said, Alma and his people gathered together all their flocks and food, and prepared to leave the Lamanites. In the morning, the Lord caused a deep sleep to come upon all their guards and while they slept, Alma's followers hurried away into the wilderness. They traveled all day and at night came to a valley which they named after Alma, because he had led them out of bondage. So grateful were they, that there in the valley they offered their thanks to the Lord for his mercy to them. Not only did the parents do so, but even the little children, as many as were able to speak, thanked the Lord for their deliverance.

The Lord spoke to Alma again, "Haste thee, and get thee and this people out of this land, for the Lamanites are awake and do pursue thee; therefore get thee out of this land, and I will stop the Lamanites in this valley, that they come no further in pursuit of this people."

Heeding this warning, they once more began to travel, and walked for twelve days through the wilderness. At the end of this time they came to the city of Zarahemla, where King Mosiah received them with much joy.

CHAPTER TWENTY-EIGHT

King Noah Is Killed

Mosiah 19.

THE PEOPLE in Noah's kingdom began to hate their king because of his wickedness. He made them pay heavy taxes, and then wasted the money, and this also angered them. Many began to murmur against him, and some of them wanted a new king.

When the army came back from searching in the forest for Alma and his followers, the people saw that it was weak, and few in numbers. This gave the people courage to rise up against King Noah. One of them was a strong man named Gideon. He decided to kill the king. He drew his sword and went out to look for him.

When he found him, the two began to fight. Gideon, being so strong, overpowered the king, and was about to kill him, when Noah turned and ran away from him. There was a high tower in the city from which the Nephites could watch for their enemies the Lamanites, in case they came to attack them.

Noah reached this tower, and climbed to the top of it. Gideon followed him, and was just about to climb the tower when the king looked toward the forest and saw an army of Lamanites coming toward the city.

The frightened king cried out, saying, "Gideon, spare me, for the Lamanites are upon us, and they will destroy us; yea, they will destroy my people."

The king was not as anxious about the people as he was to save himself. But Gideon spared his life. He too knew the danger of this Lamanite attack.

Hurrying down from the tower, the king told all his people to escape into the forest on the other side of the city. He started to run first and they all followed him, men, women and little children.

The Lamanites soon caught up with them and began to kill them. The frightened king then told the men who could run faster than the rest to leave the women and children behind, and save their own lives. The king with his wicked priests and some of the other men did this, leaving the women and children to the Lamanites. They ran as fast as they could into the dense forest to hide.

But there were many men who would not leave their families. They would rather stay and die with them, if they had to.

Those who stayed with their families chose from among them the most beautiful girls in the group and asked them to stand in front of them, so that when the Lamanites came, they would be pleased with their beauty and not kill them. This plan worked just as they had hoped. When the Lamanites came near and saw these lovely girls, they were charmed and did not kill them nor their families. But they did take them all captive, and carried them to the Lamanite land of Nephi.

The captured Nephites went before the king of the Lamanites and asked for mercy. The king told them that he would let them go back to their homes and farms if they would find King Noah and bring him to them. Also they must agree to pay the Lamanite king half of all they had and half of all they would earn for years to come. This was a heavy burden, but the Nephites agreed to it.

One of the sons of King Noah was among those taken prisoner by the Lamanites. He was a good young man named Limhi. He was chosen to rule over the Nephites in their slavery, and see that half of all their gold, silver, crops, animals and other property was given to the Lamanites.

Limhi did not wish to have his father killed, as the Lamanite king asked, although he knew that Noah was a wicked man.

Knowing this, Gideon sent men into the forest secretly to search for King Noah. They found the men who had followed the king when he commanded them to leave their wives and children behind and save their own lives.

These men were sorry for what they had done, and when they learned that their families were taken by the Lamanites back to the land of Nephi, they wanted to return to them. King Noah forbade them to go, and this made them so angry that they tied him to a stake, built a fire around him and burned him to death. This fulfilled the prophecy of Abinidi, who had said that the king would die the same kind of death to which he had condemned the prophet.

These angry men were about to kill the evil priests also, but they escaped into the forest. The men were getting ready to start for the land of Nephi to find their families when they met Gideon's group, who told them all that had happened and that the Lamanites had allowed them to return to their own lands if they paid them half of all they possessed.

The men were glad to hear their wives and children had not been killed, and they all returned to the land of Nephi to join them.

The Lamanites made an agreement with the Nephites that they would not kill them if they would pay tribute to them each year. King Limhi agreed to this, and his people worked hard giving half of all they earned to the Lamanites. In this way, peace came to the land.

The Lamanites were afraid that the Nephites would try to escape, and so they placed guards all about their city. But the Nephites stayed there and for two years there was no more trouble between them.

LAMANITE GIRLS CAPTURED.

CHAPTER TWENTY-NINE

Lamanite Girls Kidnaped

Mosiah 20.

THE wicked priests of Noah continued to live in the wilderness. They were ashamed to return to their wives and children in the land of Nephi. They were also afraid if they went back the Nephites would kill them. They had barely escaped with their lives at the time King Noah was slain. Having no other place to go, they lived in hiding in the forest.

Nearby was a place called Shemlon where the Lamanite girls often went to play. One day twenty-four of them were dancing there. The priests of Noah saw them, and desired them for their wives. Rushing out from their hiding place among the trees, they captured the girls and carried them deep into the forest.

When the Lamanites found that their daughters were missing, they thought that their slaves, the people of Limhi, had taken them, and became very angry.

In great rage, the king of the Lamanites sent his armies against the city of Limhi.

Limhi saw them coming as he watched from his high tower. He quickly led his soldiers out into the forest, so they could attack the Lamanites by surprise. When the Lamanites drew near, Limhi and his men fell upon them, and killed many of them. The battle became very fierce, and all the men fought savagely.

Although there were twice as many Lamanites as Nephites, the Nephites began to drive the Lamanites back. They knew they were fighting for their homes, their wives and their children, and they must win the battle, or they would all be destroyed. For this reason they fought harder than ever before.

The King of the Lamanites was badly wounded, and fell among the dead on the battlefield. His men left him there, not knowing he was still alive. But the Nephites found him, bound up his wounds, and nursed him so that he did not die. Then they carried him to their own king, Limhi. As they brought him in, they said: "Here is the king of the Lamanites; he having received a wound has fallen among their dead, and they have left him; and behold we have brought him before you, and now let us slay him."

But Limhi said, "Ye shall not slay him, but bring him hither that I may see him."

When they brought him closer, Limhi asked him, "What cause have ye to come up to war against my people? Behold, my people have not broken the oath that I made unto you. Therefore, why should ye break the oath which ye made unto my people?"

The Lamanite king then said to Limhi, "I have broken the oath because thy people did carry away the daughters of my people; therefore in my anger I did cause my people to come up to war against thy people."

Limhi had heard nothing about the girls being stolen. So he said to the Lamanite king, "I will search among my people and whosoever has done this thing shall perish."

Gideon was the king's captain. When he heard about the missing girls, he went to the king and said, "I pray thee, do not search this people, and lay not this thing to their charge. For do ye not remember the priests of thy father, whom this people sought to destroy? And are they not in the wilderness? And are not they the ones who have stolen the daughters of the Lamanites?"

Gideon then told Limhi to tell the Lamanite king what he had said about the wicked priests, so that the war would stop. He told Limhi that the Lamanites had already formed a new army and were coming against the city once more. He said they were bringing many more soldiers, and added, "There are but a few of us, and except the king doth pacify them towards us, we must perish."

He reminded the king of the prophecies of Abinidi, that unless they turned from evil, they would be destroyed. So he said, "Let us pacify the king, and we fulfil the oath which we have made unto him, for it is better that we should be in bondage than that we should lose our lives; therefore let us put a stop to the shedding of so much blood."

Limhi told the Lamanite king all that Gideon had said. He told him about his own wicked father, Noah, and his priests who had gone with him into the wilderness, and blamed these priests for stealing the daughters of the Lamanites.

The king believed what Limhi told him, and said, "Let us go forth to meet my people, without arms, and I swear unto you with an oath that my people shall not slay thy people."

The Lamanite king left the city, and met his armies as they were coming to fight the Nephites. He stopped them, and pleaded with them in behalf of the Nephites. Limhi and his people also went out to meet them, leaving their weapons behind. When they saw this, the Lamanites were satisfied and returned with their king to their own land, and once more there was peace.

But Limhi sent soldiers out to look for the wicked priests, hoping that they might be caught and punished for bringing war upon the rest of the people.

No matter where the soldiers looked, they could not find the wicked priests of King Noah, and neither did they find their wives, the Lamanite daughters.

The people of Limhi lived in great fear of another attack by the Lamanites, in spite of the promises of peace which had been made. They knew not how long they would live, nor when they might escape.

CHAPTER THIRTY

The Bondage Made Worse

Mosiah 21.

*T*HE PEOPLE of Limhi did not have peace, even though they had driven the Lamanites back, and spared the life of their king when they found him among the dead on the battlefield.

The fighting had made the Lamanites hate the Nephites even more than before. They wanted to destroy them, but their king had made a promise to Limhi that they would not fight the Nephites. For this reason they did not start war.

But they decided to make the Nephites as miserable as they could without really fighting. They began to whip them as they worked at their tasks. They made them carry heavy burdens on their backs, and drove them about like oxen or pack horses. All of this was in fulfilment of the prophecies of Abinidi, and came to them because of their wickedness.

The afflictions of the Nephites became so terrible that they began to murmur among themselves, looking for some way to overthrow their enemies. Some wanted to go to war against the Lamanites, and try to defeat them. Limhi knew that this was not wise. He persuaded them to work in peace until some other kind of relief could come. But they continued to go to him, pleading for permission to fight. At last he told them to do as they pleased.

They attacked the Lamanites who had come within their borders, determined to drive them out. But the Lamanites were stronger than they were, and beat them back and killed many of them. Those who were not harmed ran into the city for protection. Then there was great mourning for the dead. Widows wept for their husbands who had lost their lives in this battle; children cried for their fathers, and brothers mourned for brothers.

The widows wept continually. Those who sympathized with them became very angry with the Lamanites. They wanted to fight again hoping that this time they could win. They armed themselves and marched out against their enemies, but were sorely defeated. Now there were more widows and orphans because so many soldiers had been killed.

In their anger, they went out against the Lamanites a third time with the same result. More men were killed, and their families were left orphaned.

By now the Nephies were broken-hearted. They felt there was no relief for them. Their burdens were heavier than before and they mourned continually.

In this condition their hearts turned to the Lord. They remembered their sins, and began to repent. They thought of the promises made to them by the prophets, that they would prosper in the land if they served God, but they would be brought into bondage if they did not.

They also began to pray to the Lord in deep repentance. He was slow to hear their prayers, because they had been slow to hear his prophets. But as they continued to repent, and pray, the Lord did hear them, and began to soften the hearts of the Lamanites. It was not his purpose to free the Nephites from bondage yet, but he did soften the Lamanites' hearts so that they made their burdens lighter. The Lord also blessed the farms of the Nephites so that they grew more grain and their flocks and herds increased.

There were more women than men, because so many men had been lost in battle. King Limhi, seeing this, commanded that every man should give part of his crops to the families of these widows, so that they would not be hungry.

The people of Limhi were united now as they had never been before. They felt they must work together for their own protec-

87

tion against the Lamanites, and so they could better care for their farms and animals.

King Limhi kept guards about the city to protect his people from surprise attacks by the Lamanites. He also took guards with him as he went out of the city, fearing the Lamanites might try to capture him.

The city had walls around it, and no one could go in or out except through the gates where guards were stationed. Outside of these walls, the farms were situated.

The Nephites now began to notice that some of their crops were being stolen. The wicked priests of Noah were carrying their grain away. Limhi sent out soldiers to try to catch these priests, to stop them from stealing the grain and to punish them for taking the daughters of the Lamanites. But they could not find them.

Limhi kept hoping that some relief would come. He remembered that his people had come from Zarahemla, and he wished that they could return there and enjoy the protection of the main group of Nephites. He sent out scouting parties to search for the city and get help from there. But none of the scouts could find it, and returned to Limhi disappointed.

CHAPTER THIRTY-ONE

A Search for Help

Mosiah 8 and 21.

*K*ING LIMHI was determined to find a way of freeing his people from their bondage to the Lamanites. He knew he would find friends in Zarahemla if his scouts could only find that city. He also felt sure that the people there would send men to help him if they knew what had happened.

Although his scouts had searched for the city before and had failed to find it, the king now decided to send out another group. He called forty-three of his best men to him, and commanded them to go again and try to find Zarahemla.

These men left as the king commanded. They soon lost their way, and for a time were not sure even how to return to their own homes. But they continued on, looking for some sign of the Nephite city.

In their travels one day they came into a land where there were lakes and rivers. They also found ruins of houses and other buildings, and then the dried bones of thousands of people who had been killed in a war. There were also bones of many animals.

They saw, too, the swords and breastplates which had been used in the battle. They carried some of these with them to show King Limhi. The hilts of the swords had rotted away, because so many years had passed since the battle took place in which these people were killed. The blades of the swords were rusty too, but the breastplates which had been worn by these soldiers were not rusty for they were made of copper and brass, which do not rust.

Then to their great surprise they found twenty-four plates of gold, which were covered with engravings. These plates resembled those which King Limhi had, and on which was a record of all that had taken place in the reigns of Limhi, wicked King Noah, and Zeniff who had led them into the land where their homes were now located.

They picked up these gold plates, and planned to take them to King Limhi, along with the weapons they had found.

They continued to travel and at last found their way back to the city of Limhi. But they did not find Zarahemla.

As soon as they got home, they went to the king and told him of their travels. They were sorry they could not find Zarahemla. But the king was very interested in their story about the land of ruined houses and slain soldiers. They showed him the weapons which they had brought back and also gave to him the gold plates. When Limhi looked at the engravings on the plates he could not read them, because they were in a language which he could not understand.

The king listened to all his scouts told him. As they told their story, he believed that it was Zarahemla which they had found. He thought the city had been destroyed and all its inhabitants killed. He was mistaken in this, for the city of Zarahemla was still standing, and the people there were wondering about him and his people.

CHAPTER THIRTY-TWO

The Lord Brings Help

Mosiah 7.

THE PEOPLE of Limhi continued to humble themselves before the Lord in prayer, asking for freedom from slavery. At last the Lord was ready to answer their prayers and bring them help.

In the city of Zarahemla, the relatives and friends of those who had followed Zeniff into the wilderness wondered what had become of them.

They continually went to King Mosiah asking him to send out a searching party to find them. At first Mosiah refused, but when the people came so often with the same request, at last he consented. He called sixteen strong men to make the search.

Their leader's name was Ammon. He was a descendant of Zarahemla, the founder of the city. Ammon led his men into the forest. He knew he was to go to the land of Nephi, but he did not know the course they should take. He and his men were soon lost in the wilderness. They wandered about for forty days, and then came to a hill which was near the land of Nephi. Although they did not know it, the Lord had been leading them in the right direction.

Leaving most of his men on this hill, Ammon took three of them with him, and went down into the land of Nephi. He did not know whether he would find friend or foe. There were many Lamanites in that region.

Soon they saw a city, and walked toward it. Before they reached it, they met the king with a group of soldiers.

It was King Limhi and his guards. They quickly surrounded Ammon and his three companions, bound them securely, and carried them into the city where they put them in prison.

At the time Ammon was captured, Limhi and his soldiers were outside of the city, as they often were, guarding the farms and looking for the priests of Noah. It was against the law of Limhi for anyone to come near the gates of the city when the king and his guards were outside. For this reason, Ammon and his men were arrested. Limhi had no way of knowing at first whether Ammon was a friend or an enemy, and he thought these men might even be some of the wicked priests.

After Ammon and his three companions had been left in prison for two days, they were brought before King Limhi to be questioned. They still were bound tightly as they stood before the king.

King Limhi told Ammon that he was a son of Noah, who was the son of Zeniff, who had led the people from Zarahemla into the land of Nephi. Then he said, "And now I desire to know the cause whereby ye were so bold as to come near the walls of the city when I, myself, was with my guards without the gate? And now for this cause have I suffered that ye should be preserved that I might inquire of you, or else I should have caused that my guards should have put you to death. Ye are now permitted to speak."

Ammon's feet were untied, but his hands were left bound. He walked toward the throne, and bowed before the king. When he arose, he said, "O king, I am very thankful before God this day that I am yet alive, and am permitted to speak, and I will endeavor to speak with boldness. For I am assured that if ye had known me ye would not have suffered that I should have worn these bands. For I am Ammon and am a descendant of Zarahemla, and have come up out of the land of Zarahemla to inquire concerning our brethren whom Zeniff brought up out of that land."

When Limhi heard this he was overjoyed. He was glad to learn that his relatives and friends in Zarahemla were yet alive, and were not destroyed in the land which his scouts had found. He also rejoiced because he felt help had come at last, and he and his people would be freed from their bondage to the Lamanites.

He said he would call his people together the next day, so they too could meet Ammon. Then he told Ammon they were slaves to the Lamanites, and that they had to give the Lamanites half of all they owned or raised.

Remembering that Ammon and his companions were still tied, the king commanded his guards to set them free. He also sent to the hill to bring the rest of Ammon's men. They cared for them, because they were weak from hunger because of their long journey.

There was great rejoicing in the palace, and Ammon and his friends were given the best Limhi had. Limhi told them how he hoped they would lead his people to freedom. He said they would be glad even to be slaves of the Nephites in Zarahemla, for, he said, it would be better to be in bondage to them than to the Lamanites.

CHAPTER THIRTY-THREE

The People Rejoice

Mosiah 7, 8 and 21.

*K*ING LIMHI called all his people together the next day, and told them of the coming of Ammon. He said, "O ye my people, lift up your heads and be comforted, for behold the time is at hand or is not far distant when we shall no longer be in subjection to our enemies. * * * Therefore, lift up your heads and rejoice, and put your trust in God."

He told them how the Lord long ago had brought the children of Israel out of bondage in Egypt and had caused them to walk through the Red Sea on dry land. He had fed them manna in the wilderness, so that they did not starve. He believed the Lord would help them escape also.

He told them that their bondage had come to them because they had sinned and forgotten the Lord. He related what had happened to the Prophet Abinidi. He mentioned Abinidi's teachings, and how he had warned them that the Lord would send his judgments on them if they did not repent. He reminded them also of Abinidi's prophecy that Jesus would come as the Savior.

Limhi explained what Ammon had said about the people of Zarahemla, and then asked Ammon to stand up before them. Ammon told them all that had happened in Zarahemla since Zeniff had left the city. He explained the teachings of the good King Benjamin who had taught the people to love each other, to care for the poor and needy, and to serve the Lord.

At the close of the meeting, the king sent his people back to their homes. Then he brought out the plates on which the record of his own people had been kept from the time Zeniff left Zarahemla, and allowed Ammon to read them.

As soon as Ammon had finished with the record, the king asked him if he could interpret other languages. Ammon said he could not. The king then told him about the twenty-four plates which his scouts had found in the valley of the dry bones. He said, "There is no one in the land that is able to interpret the language or the engravings that are on the plates. Therefore I said unto thee, 'Canst thou translate?' "

The king was disappointed that Ammon could not read the strange language. But he asked still further, "Knowest thou of any one that can translate? For I am desirous that these records should be translated into our language, for perhaps they will give us a knowledge of a remnant of the people who have been destroyed from whence these records came."

Ammon did know of a man who could translate, and said to the king, "I can assuredly tell thee, O king, of a man that can translate the records: for he has wherewith that he can look and translate all records that are of ancient date, and it is a gift from God."

He told the king that the instruments through which the translation was made were called "interpreters," and said that no one could look through them unless he was commanded to do so by the Lord, or he would die.

"And behold," he continued, "the king of the people who is in the land of Zarahemla is the man that is commanded to do these things, and who has this high gift from God."

King Limhi hoped that when he and his people were freed from the Lamanites, he could take these records to King Mosiah in Zarahemla, and have them translated.

Limhi told Ammon the story of their bondage, and of their wars with the Lamanites in an effort to be free. Ammon mourned for the dead who had been killed in these wars. He was also filled with sorrow over the death of Abinidi.

The people of Limhi rejoiced at the coming of Ammon. They also made a covenant with the Lord that they would serve him, and many of them wished to be baptized. Limhi the king also desired baptism, and he asked Ammon if he would baptize them all.

They remembered how Alma had led some of the people into the wilderness and baptized them. They desired to do as the people of Alma had done, and many of them were now sorry they had not followed Alma.

Although Ammon was a good man, he did not perform baptisms. He did not feel that he was worthy to do so.

Because no one in the city of Limhi had authority to baptize, they did not at that time organize a branch of the Church.

CHAPTER THIRTY-FOUR

The Escape

Mosiah 22.

*L*IMHI and Ammon began to plan to lead their people out of bondage. The king called everyone in the city into a meeting to talk it over. He allowed each person to offer a plan of escape, if he wished to do so.

No one could think of any way except to take their families and flocks into the wilderness, and hurry out of the land before the Lamanites knew they were missing. They were not able to do this before, because they had no one to guide them to Zarahemla. But now Ammon would show them the way. They did not wish to fight the Lamanites because so many of their men had already been killed in their wars, leaving them few in number.

Gideon, the captain of the army, who had helped the king out of trouble before, now stood up in the meeting and said, "O king, thou hast hitherto hearkened unto my words many times when we have been contending with our brethren the Lamanites. And now, O king, if thou hast not found me to be an unprofitable servant, or if thou hast hitherto listened to my words in any degree, and they have been of service to thee, even so I desire that thou wouldst listen to my words at this time, and I will be thy servant and deliver this people out of bondage."

The king told him to speak, and Gideon said: "Behold the back pass, through the back wall on the back side of the city. The guards of the Lamanites by night are drunken; therefore let us send a proclamation among all this people that they might gather together their flocks and herds, that they might drive them into the wilderness by night. And I will go according to thy command, and pay the last tribute of wine to the Lamanites, and they will be drunken, and we will pass through the secret pass on the

97

left of the camp when they are drunken and asleep. Thus we will depart with our women and our children, our flocks and our herds into the wilderness, and we will travel around the land of Shilom."

The king agreed to Gideon's plan. He commanded his people to be ready to leave on a certain night. Gideon took wine which the people were forced to make for the Lamanites, and brought it to the guards at the gate. The guards drank much of the wine, and became drunk, and slept soundly for many hours.

With Ammon as their leader, the people then went out through the gates, past the sleeping guards. They found the secret pass, and started for the land of Zarahemla. They took food to last them through the journey, and as many of their other possessions as they could carry.

When the Lamanites found that the people of Limhi had escaped, they sent an army after them. They followed their trail for two days but after that they had to give up the pursuit.

After many days of travel, Ammon brought Limhi and his followers to the city of Zarahemla, where King Mosiah received them with much joy.

There they also met their friends who had followed Alma into the wilderness to escape from the wicked King Noah, the father of Limhi. Alma had led them safely to Zarahemla, although for a time the Lamanites held them also in bondage, as related in an earlier story.

Soon after their arrival there, Limhi gave Mosiah the plates telling of the history of his own people, and also the twenty-four gold plates taken from the valley of dry bones.

One day Mosiah called all his people together and read to them the story of the people of Limhi from the time Zeniff had taken them into the wilderness until their arrival back in Zarahemla. He also read the story of Alma and his escape from Noah. Alma was called upon to speak, and he told the people that they must remember that it was only through the help of the Lord that they were able to escape, and he told them they must always serve God.

Limhi and his people still desired to be baptized, so Alma took them to the water and there baptized them all.

Alma then established branches of the Church in all parts of the land of Zarahemla, appointing members of the priesthood to preside in each branch.

So many people joined the Church that it was necessary for Alma to organize many branches or congregations, and appoint teachers and priests to take charge of the meetings held among them.

Alma guided the work, and performed many baptisms, just as he had done while near the waters of Mormon in the wilderness.

CHAPTER THIRTY-FIVE

Alma the Younger

Mosiah 27.

ALMA and King Mosiah taught the people to love each other and live peacefully together. There were four groups in the city now, those who established the city of Zarahemla, the Nephites who followed the first King Mosiah to the city, the people Alma brought there, and those who came with King Limhi.

Many were willing to do as Alma and Mosiah asked, but some of the young people refused. They committed many sins and rejected the Lord and his servants.

Alma's son, whose name was also Alma, was one of them. He was a leader among these wicked people. Four of his companions were sons of King Mosiah. Together with Alma, they went from place to place, urging the people not to follow the advice of their own fathers, but to live wicked lives if they felt like it.

Alma the younger was a clever speaker. He flattered the people, and became a great grievance to his own father and to the king. Some of the people, believing his lying words, were led astray.

Alma went to the Lord in prayer, asking him to soften the hearts of these young men that they might be converted to the gospel, and use their great powers for good rather than for evil.

One day as the younger Alma and the four sons of Mosiah were going about, trying to destroy the Church, an angel came down from heaven, and appeared to them in a cloud of light. When he spoke, his voice sounded like thunder, and shook the earth where the young men stood.

Alma and his companions were so frightened when he came that they fell to the earth. The angel said, "Alma, arise and stand forth, for why persecutest thou the church of God?"

100

The angel then said, "The Lord hath heard the prayers of his people and also the prayers of his servant Alma, who is thy father; for he has prayed with much faith concerning thee that thou mightest be brought to a knowledge of the truth. Therefore for this purpose have I come to convince thee of the power and authority of God that the prayers of his servants might be answered according to their faith."

The earth continued to shake as he spoke. And he reminded Alma of this. "Now behold," he said, "can ye dispute the power of God? Doth not my voice shake the earth? And can ye not also behold me before you? And I am sent from God."

He commanded Alma to stop fighting against the Church, and then he disappeared.

Alma and Mosiah's sons again fell to the earth, being overcome by the visit of the angel. They were greatly surprised at what they had heard and seen.

Alma was so overcome that he was not able to speak, and he became so weak that he could neither walk, nor even raise his hand. His friends, seeing his condition, carefully picked him up, and carried him to his father, telling him all that had happened.

The father was grateful, because he knew now that God had heard his prayers in behalf of his son. He called in the people of the city so that they might see the result of the prayers which had been offered up. Then he asked those who held the priesthood to fast and pray with him in behalf of his son, that he might be given his speech and that he might be made strong and well once more.

They fasted and prayed for two days and two nights, and then strength came back to Alma's son. His speech also returned, and seeing the people around him, he began to speak to them, telling them that the Lord had shown him what a great sin he had committed in fighting the Church. He said that although he had denied that Jesus was the Savior, now he knew that the Lord was the son of God, and would come into the world.

He was completely changed. He no longer fought against the Church, but tried to build it up. The sons of Mosiah were also converted by the visit of the angel. They and the young Alma together now went to all the places where they had been before, and tried to overcome the harm they had done in their first visits when they lied to the people. They told about their conversion and admitted their former sins.

The Saints were thankful for this change. But many of the wicked people would not believe what the boys said, and they began to persecute them, even though persecution was against the law. In spite of this the young men kept on preaching their gospel to all who would listen.

CHAPTER THIRTY-SIX

The Sons of Mosiah

Mosiah 28.

*J*HE FOUR SONS of Mosiah who had been converted with Alma were now loyal missionaries for the Church. Wherever they went, they preached the gospel.

One day they came to their father the king, asking his permission to go on a mission to the Lamanites. They wished not only to bring the gospel to those warlike people, but they believed that if the Lamanites were converted, hatred would be taken out of their hearts, and they would stop fighting against the Nephites.

Mosiah was not sure what to do. He was growing old, and knew that before long, it would be necessary for him to turn the affairs of the kingdom over to one of his sons. This he could not do unless the boys were home. He also feared for their lives, knowing as he did how fierce and cruel the Lamanites were.

None of his sons wanted to be king in his place. They said they would much prefer to go on their mission to the Lamanites. The king still hesitated; and the boys kept on pleading with him.

Finally he made it a matter of prayer. In answer the Lord spoke to him and said, "Let them go up, for many shall believe on their words and they shall have eternal life, and I will deliver thy sons out of the hands of the Lamanites."

With this assurance of protection from the Lord, Mosiah told his sons they could go on their mission. The boys were happy, and prepared to leave.

Mosiah at first did not know what to do about his kingdom. He sent out word among the people asking them whom they would like to be king after he died, and they said they desired his son Aaron. But Aaron was filled with zeal and would rather be a

BOOK OF MORMON STORIES FOR YOUNG LATTER-DAY SAINTS

humble missionary to the Lamanites than to be king over the land of Zarahemla.

While he was wondering what he should do, King Mosiah remembered the twenty-four plates which had been brought to him by King Limhi. He now decided to translate them, and see what they contained.

Using his "interpreters," he studied the ancient writings on the plates of gold. They told the story of the brother of Jared and the people he led to America; and of the wars of these people. They described the last great battle in which all were killed but Coriantumr, who finally wandered to the city of Zarahemla where he died.

The dried bones found by the people of Limhi were those of the Jaredites who had been killed in their last great war. The gold plates which they found, and which now told the story of their destruction, were those which were closed up by Ether, the last Jaredite prophet.

When Mosiah told his people about the translation of the record, they mourned for the great Jaredite nation which had been destroyed.

After completing the translation, Mosiah took these plates, and all the others which he had, and turned them over to Alma, the younger, asking him to be the record-keeper of the Nephites.

Alma's father was now more than eighty years old, and could no longer carry on his work. Calling his son to him one day, he appointed him to preside over the Church in Zarahemla. Shortly after this, he died, and his son, Alma the younger, carried on the work in his place.

CHAPTER THIRTY-SEVEN

The People Rule Themselves

Mosiah 29.

*M*OSIAH asked his son Aaron if he would be the next king of Zarahemla. Aaron refused. He desired so much to be a missionary to the Lamanites that he did not wish to be king.

Mosiah feared that if some other man were appointed, trouble might come. Aaron was the one who was entitled to rule. Although he had been converted by the angel who appeared to young Alma, Mosiah thought that some time Aaron might return to his bad habits. If he did, and someone else was on the throne which could have been his, he might start a war to get it back.

Mosiah also feared that if a person not of the royal family were chosen, some men in the land might feel they had as much right to the throne as he did, and they also might start a war.

With these things in mind, Mosiah wrote a message to his people which said that if a wicked man became their ruler, he would cause the people to sin, and then trouble would come upon them all.

"Now let us be wise," the king wrote, "and look forward to these things, and do that which will make for the peace of this people. Therefore," he said, "I will be your king the remainder of my days; nevertheless, let us appoint judges to judge this people according to our law."

He told the people to hold an election, and vote for the men they desired as governors. In this way they could rule themselves, and would no longer be subject to a king.

"Therefore," he said, "choose you by the voice of this people, judges that ye may be judged according to the laws which have been given to you by our fathers, which are correct, and which were given them by the hand of the Lord."

Mosiah taught a great truth to the people at this time. He said, "It is not common that the voice of the people desireth anything contrary to that which is right; but it is common for the lesser part of the people to desire that which is not right. Therefore, this shall ye observe and make it your law, to do your business by the voice of the people. And if the time comes that the voice of the people doth choose iniquity, then is the time that the judgments of God will come upon you."

He said that all the people in the land should have equal rights, and be free.

The people believed what Mosiah wrote to them, and agreed to have equal rights for all. They held an election which he had suggested, and in this way chose the judges or governors of the people. They loved Mosiah even more than before because of what he had now told them. They saw that indeed he was a good man, and did not wish to be unjust to anyone.

Alma, the young man who had taken his father's place as high priest, was elected to the office of chief judge, so he was now both chief judge to rule the land, and the presiding high priest in the Church.

Soon after this, King Mosiah died. Five hundred and nine years had passed since Lehi and his family had left Jerusalem.

CHAPTER THIRTY-EIGHT

The Mission to the Lamanites

Alma 17.

A SHORT TIME after the election of the judges, or governors, in the land of Zarahemla, the sons of Mosiah prepared for their mission to the Lamanites. Their father, King Mosiah, had been told by the Lord to allow them to go, and that many would believe their teachings.

The four boys fasted and prayed a great deal, asking the Lord to guide and help them on this mission. They prayed to be instruments in the hands of the Lord in teaching the Lamanites the gospel, and also the truth about the Nephites.

They said goodbye to their father, and left the city on a mission which was to last fourteen years. They took with them swords, bows and arrows and sling shots, so that they could kill game for food on their way.

They traveled in the wilderness for many days, and continued to fast and pray for help and guidance. One day the Lord spoke to them and said, "Be comforted." And they were comforted.

Later the Lord spoke to them once more, and said, "Go forth among the Lamanites, thy brethren, and establish my word; yet ye shall be patient in long suffering and afflictions, that ye may show forth good examples unto them in me; and I will make an instrument of thee in my hands unto the salvation of many souls."

The boys were happy with this revelation from the Lord. It gave them new courage for their missions. They did not fear any longer. They knew that if they did what was right the Lord would help them.

When they reached the borders of the Lamanite country, they stopped to discuss their future plans. They decided that instead of all going together, they should separate, and go in different directions. Ammon, their leader, blessed each of his brothers and gave them instructions. Then bidding each other goodbye and trusting in the Lord to bring them together at some future time, they separated, each one going into a different part of the land.

They felt they had undertaken a great work, and it was great, "for they had undertaken to preach the word of God to a wild and a hardened people and a ferocious people; a people who delighted in murdering the Nephites and robbing and plundering them; and their hearts were set upon riches, or upon gold and silver, and precious stones; yet they sought to obtain these by murdering and plundering, that they might not labor for them with their own hands.

"Thus they were a very indolent people, many of whom did worship idols and the curse of God had fallen upon them because of the traditions of their fathers; notwithstanding the promises of the Lord were extended to them on conditions of repentance."

CHAPTER THIRTY-NINE

Ammon Saves the Sheep

Alma 17.

*L*EAVING his brothers to go their various ways, Ammon went into a land called Ishmael, named after the sons of Ishmael, who were also Lamanites. Ishmael was one of the men who came with Lehi from Jerusalem.

No sooner had Ammon reached there, than he was captured by the Lamanites who bound him and carried him to their king. This was the custom of the Lamanites whenever they found any Nephites in their land. They did it so that the king could decide whether to kill these captives, put them in prison, make slaves of them, or drive them back into the Nephite country.

The name of this Lamanite ruler was Lamoni, a descendant of Ishmael. The king asked Ammon why he had come into that land, and if it was his desire to live among the Lamanites.

Ammon said, "Yea, I desire to dwell among this people for a time; yea, and perhaps until the day I die."

This pleased Lamoni, who ordered his men to cut the ropes which bound Ammon. The king learned to like Ammon and offered to give him one of his daughters for his wife. Ammon did not wish to be married at this time, so he said, "Nay, but I will be thy servant." And so it was.

The king gave him the task of herding his sheep. Three days later Ammon and some of the king's servants were driving the sheep to water. Other Lamanites who also brought their own sheep to this same place became angry. As the king's flocks approached, these other men began to drive them away so that they could not get near the water.

The servants who were with Ammon became frightened, and said, "Now the king will slay us, as he has our brethren, because their flocks were scattered by the wickedness of these men."

Then they began to weep, and they said, "Our flocks are scattered already."

When Ammon saw this, he was glad because he knew that he would now be able to use the power which the Lord had given him, and it would make an opportunity for him to begin preaching the gospel to the Lamanites.

Ammon comforted his fellow servants, and said, "My brethren, be of good cheer and let us go in search of the flocks and we will gather them together and bring them back unto the place of water; and thus we will preserve the flocks unto the king and he will not slay us."

Ammon and his friends then gathered up the sheep, and headed them back to the water hole. Again the wicked men came out to scatter them, but Ammon told the king's servants to surround the sheep, and keep them close together in one herd while he went alone to fight these enemies.

The king's servants did as Ammon told them, and herded the sheep close together, and kept them there. They watched Ammon as he went out against their enemies. When the wicked men saw him coming, they thought they could easily kill him.

They began throwing stones at Ammon, but they could not hit him. Then Ammon took out his own sling shot, and six of his enemies were killed by his stones. Seeing this, the others became very angry at Ammon, and were still more determined to kill him. When they could not hit him with their stones, they came at him all together with clubs, planning to beat him to death.

Ammon was not afraid. As they came close, he drew his sword, and when the men raised their arms to strike him with their clubs, Ammon cut off their arms. The only man he killed with his sword was their leader.

When the rest of the men saw their leader die and others having their arms cut off as they tried to club Ammon, they ran away. Ammon chased them, but soon returned and helped the

AMMON SAVES THE SHEEP.

other servants of the king to water the sheep. Then they went back to the city.

They carried with them the severed arms of their enemies, and laid them before the king and told him what had happened. Ammon did not go in with them. He stayed out and fed the king's horses.

The king was greatly impressed by the story of the other servants as they explained how Ammon had saved the flocks, and as they told of his great power in fighting the enemies of the king. Especially was he surprised to learn that the enemies who attacked them were not able to hurt or to kill Ammon.

None of his servants had been as faithful to him as Ammon was, and although he was surprised to learn of Ammon's power, he was pleased to know that Ammon was so dependable.

CHAPTER FORTY

The Great Spirit

Alma 18.

THE INDIANS of America called God the Great Spirit. Many of our western scouts learned this as they traveled among them, and so did the Utah Pioneers as they made friends with the Indians after coming to the valleys of the mountains.

This custom of speaking of God as the Great Spirit has been common among the Indians for many years. Even in ancient times in America, the Lamanites spoke of the Lord in this way.

When King Lamoni heard his servants tell how Ammon had protected the sheep from their enemies, and how the wicked men were not able to hurt him, Lamoni said, "Surely, this is more than a man. Behold is not this the Great Spirit?" He thought that Ammon was the Lord, who had come among them.

His servants answered by saying, "Whether he be the Great Spirit or a man, we know not; but this much we do know, that he cannot be slain by the enemies of the king; neither can they scatter the king's flocks when he is with us, because of his expertness and great strength. Therefore, we know that he is a friend to the king. And now, O king, we do not believe that a man has such great power, for we know he cannot be slain."

When the king heard this he said, "Now I know that it is the Great Spirit and he has come down at this time to preserve your lives, that I might not slay you as I did your brethren. Now this is the Great Spirit of whom our fathers have spoken."

King Lamoni became very frightened, because he had killed many of his servants who were not able to prevent the sheep from being scattered. He wondered if the Great Spirit was about to punish him for doing this.

Turning once more to his servants, he asked, "Where is this man that has such great power?"

They told him he was out feeding the horses. Before he had sent his servants out to drive the sheep to water, he had also told them to feed the horses and prepare the chariots so that he could leave for the land of Nephi where he was to attend a feast being held by the Lamanites. The father of Lamoni, who was king over all of the Lamanites, was giving the feast.

When Lamoni heard that Ammon was out feeding the horses and getting them ready for this journey he was even more surprised because of Ammon's faithfulness, and said, "Surely there has not been any servant among all my servants that has been so faithful as this man; for even he doth remember all my commandments to execute them. Now I surely know that this is the Great Spirit, and I would desire him that he come in unto me, but I durst not."

Ammon finished his work with the horses and chariots, and came into the palace to tell the king they were ready for the journey. As he came inside the room, he saw a strange look on the king's face, so he went back out again.

Another of the servants ran to him and said, "Rabbanah, the king desireth thee to stay."

The word *rabbanah* means "powerful man," or "great king." This servant, believing Ammon was some very great man, if not the Great Spirit, called him by this name as a mark of respect.

Ammon went back into the palace, and asked the king, "What wilt thou that I should do for thee?"

The king was still frightened, and was so afraid of Ammon that for an hour he did not speak. He did not know what he should say to Ammon.

As time went on, Ammon again asked what the king desired of him, but still the king did not talk. The Spirit of the Lord then came upon Ammon, so that he was able to read the king's thoughts, and he said:

"Is it because that thou hast heard that I defended thy servants and thy flocks, and slew seven of their brethren with the sling and with the sword, and smote off the arms of others, in order to defend thy flocks and thy servants; behold is it this that causeth thy marvelings? I say unto you, what is it, that thy marvelings are so great? Behold, I am a man, and am thy servant. Therefore, whatsoever thou desirest which is right, that will I do."

When the king heard this, he marveled again, for he knew that Ammon had read his thoughts. The king now began to speak. The first thing he said was, "Who art thou? Art thou that Great Spirit who knows all things?"

Ammon replied and said, "I am not."

The king then asked, "How knowest thou the thoughts of my heart? Thou mayest speak boldly and tell me concerning these things; and also tell me by what power ye slew and smote off the arms of my brethren that scatteterd my flocks. If thou wilt tell me these things, whatsoever thou desirest I will give unto thee. And if it were needed, I would guard thee with my armies, but I know that thou art more powerful than all they. Nevertheless, whatsoever thou desirest of me I will grant it unto thee."

Ammon was a wise man. He knew that the power that he possessed had come from God, and that only through the Lord was he able to do what he had done. He also knew that it was because of the blessings of the Lord that King Lamoni now asked him these questions.

He asked the king if he would believe what he taught. The king said, "Yea, I will believe all thy words."

Ammon then asked, "Believest thou that there is a God?"

The king said, "I do not know what that meaneth."

Then Ammon said, "Believest thou that there is a Great Spirit?"

The king said, "Yea."

Ammon explained that God is the Great Spirit, and that he created the world and all that is in it. He told him that God lives in heaven, with his angels, and that he watches people on earth, and knows all their thoughts, and all of their intentions.

Lamoni then asked, "Art thou sent from God?"

Ammon told him that he was, but that he was just a man who had been blessed with the power and spirit of the Lord. He then told Lamoni about Lehi, and the long journey to America. He told him the truth about the rebellion of Laman and Lemuel and the sons of Ishmael. He then spoke of the Savior, Jesus Christ, saying he would soon come into the world to save his people.

The king believed what Ammon taught and began to pray to the Lord, saying, "O Lord, have mercy, according to thy abundant mercy which thou hast had upon the people of Nephi, have upon me and my people."

When he finished this prayer, he fainted, and fell to the earth as if he were dead.

His servants picked him up and laid him upon a bed. He was unconscious there for two days and two nights, and his wife and children mourned over him, thinking he had passed away.

CHAPTER FORTY-ONE

A Great Conversion

Alma 19.

*T*HE PEOPLE of Lamoni thought their king was dead. They mourned for him as they made a sepulchre and prepared to hold his funeral.

Before she would allow the king to be buried, the queen asked to talk with Ammon. She had heard about the wonderful things he did, and so she sent for him.

When he came before her, she said, "The servants of my husband have made it known unto me that thou art a prophet of a holy God, and that thou hast power to do many mighty works in his name. Therefore, if this is the case, I would that ye should go in and see my husband, for he has been laid upon his bed for the space of two days and two nights, and some say that he is not dead. But others say that he is dead."

This was what Ammon desired. He knew that Lamoni was under the power of the Lord, that the darkness of his mind was being taken away and in its place the light of the Holy Spirit was coming upon him.

Doing as the queen said, he went in and saw the king as he lay upon his bed. Ammon knew the king was not dead, and he said to the queen, "He is not dead, but sleepeth in God. And on the morrow he shall rise again. Therefore, bury him not. Believest thou this?"

The queen replied, "I have had no witness save thy word and the word of our servants. Nevertheless I believe that it shall be according as thou hast said."

Ammon was happy to hear her say this. He said, "Blessed art thou because of thy exceeding faith. For I say unto thee, woman, there has not been such great faith among all the people of the Nephites."

Believing what Ammon said, the queen now waited for her husband to arise. She watched at his bedside until the next day, and then, just as Ammon had said, the king arose. Opening his eyes he saw his wife by his side, and reached out his hand to her, and said, "Blessed be the name of God, and blessed art thou. For as sure as thou livest, I have seen my Redeemer, and he shall come forth and be born of a woman, and he shall redeem all mankind who believe on his name."

His heart was filled with joy. After saying this, the king was again overpowered by the Spirit of the Lord, and fell back upon his bed, unconscious. The queen was then filled with the spirit, and she too was overcome, and fell down with her husband.

Ammon was grateful for the conversion which was coming to the king and the queen. He knelt down and prayed to the Lord, offering his thanks for answering his prayers and bringing faith to the Lamanites. As he did so, the Spirit of the Lord came upon him in such power that he too was overcome, and fell down unconscious with the king and queen.

When the king's servants saw all three of them lying there, they became very frightened, and started to cry out to the Lord. They were the servants who had been with Ammon and seen his wonderful deeds, and they believed what Ammon said. The Spirit of the Lord now came upon them, and they too were overcome and fell to the earth unconscious.

One of the servants of the queen was a woman who had believed in the Lord for many years. She had been converted by a wonderful vision which had been given to her father. When she saw what had happened to the king and queen, Ammon and the other servants, she knew that the power of the Lord had brought it about. She thought that if the people of the city could see this wonderful thing they might be converted to the Lord.

117

Running outside, she called to all who were near, and asked them to come to the palace. Many came, and stood watching those who were lying there. But the people did not understand. Some said a great evil had come to the palace, because the king had allowed Ammon, a Nephite, to live in the city.

Others said that the king had brought this evil upon his own house because he had killed so many of his servants when the sheep were scattered by his enemies.

Among those who were there were some of the men who had been at the water holes when Ammon had fought against the enemies of the king as they scattered the sheep. A brother of one of those who had been killed, came in. When he saw Ammon lying there, helpless, he thought it was an opportunity to kill him in revenge. He drew his sword and walked over to where Ammon lay. As he raised his arm to kill Ammon, the Lord smote him, and he dropped dead.

When the people saw this, they became frightened, and some believed that Ammon was the Great Spirit. Others said he had been sent by the Great Spirit. The more wicked among them rebuked those who spoke like that, and said Ammon was a monster who had been sent by the Nephites to torment the Lamanites. But the righteous believed that Ammon was sent by the Great Spirit to punish them for their many sins.

This started a quarrel which became very bitter. The woman who had gathered the people together was disappointed, because she thought they would be converted when they saw the king and the others lying there, overcome by the Spirit of the Lord.

In tears, she went into the room where the queen lay. She knelt down, and took the queen's hand, thinking she could raise her from the ground.

The queen awoke and arose, and said with a loud voice, "O blessed Jesus. O blessed God, have mercy on this people."

She turned and took King Lamoni by the hand, and he too

arose. Seeing his people arguing there in the palace, he rebuked them, and told them what Ammon had taught.

Many believed what the king said, and were converted. But others would not believe. They turned and left the palace.

Ammon now arose, as did the servants, whose hearts had been turned to righteousness while they were overcome by the Spirit of the Lord.

Those who had been blessed in this way, went out and taught others in the city. Many of these believed also.

Ammon knew that the believers must now be baptized. He took them down into the water, and baptized them. Then he organized a branch of the Church among them, and the Lord blessed all the members.

CHAPTER FORTY-TWO

Ammon Saves His Brethren

Alma 20.

KING LAMONI wished to have his father meet Ammon. His father was the ruler of all the Lamanites. Lamoni and certain other men ruled parts of the land, but they had to obey the old king who governed them all.

Lamoni asked Ammon to go with him to the land of Nephi where his father lived. But the voice of the Lord came to Ammon and told him he must not go there for the old king would try to kill him. Instead, the Lord said that Ammon's brethren had been taken by some of the wicked Lamanites, and put in prison. Ammon was instructed by the Lord to go and set them free.

On hearing this Ammon went to Lamoni, and told him he could not go to the land of Nephi to see the old king, but that he must go to Middoni instead, for there his brothers were in prison, and he must set them free.

Lamoni said, "I know in the strength of the Lord thou canst do all things. But behold I will go with thee to the land of Middoni for the king of the land of Middoni, whose name is Antiomno, is a friend unto me; therefore I go to the land of Middoni that I may flatter the king of the land, and he will cast thy brethren out of prison."

Then Lamoni asked Ammon, "Who told thee that thy brethren were in prison?"

Ammon replied, "No one hath told me save it be God; and he said unto me, Go and deliver thy brethren, for they are in prison in the land of Middoni."

When Lamoni heard this, he sent his servants to make ready the horses and chariots, and then said to Ammon, "Come, I will go with thee down to the land of Middoni, and there I will plead with the king that he will cast thy brethren out of prison."

Soon Ammon and Lamoni started their journey. On the way they met Lamoni's father, the king of all the land. They stopped their horses, and the old king asked his son why he had not come to the feast he had prepared.

The father was angry when he saw that Ammon was a Nephite, and asked Lamoni, "Whither art thou going with this Nephite?"

Lamoni was afraid to offend his father, but he felt it best to tell him all that had happened since the coming of Ammon. It made the old king angry. When Lamoni told him that he and Ammon were going to the land of Middoni to free Ammon's brethren, the old king became more angry than ever, and said:

"Lamoni, thou art going to deliver these Nephites, who are sons of a liar. Behold he robbed our fathers, and now his children are also come amongst us that they may, by their cunning and their lyings, deceive us, that they again may rob us of our property."

The old king was telling some of the untruths which the Lamanites had taught their children for many years.

In his anger, the king told his son Lamoni to draw his sword and kill Ammon, and return with him to his own land.

Lamoni said to his father, "I will not slay Ammon, neither will I return to the land of Ishmael, but I go to the land of Middoni that I may release the brethren of Ammon, for I know they are just men and holy prophets of the true God."

When his father heard this, he drew his own sword intending to kill Lamoni. But Ammon stopped the old king, and said, "Behold thou shalt not slay thy son. * * * If thou shouldst slay thy son, he being an innocent man, his blood would cry from the

121

ground to the Lord his God for vengeance to come upon thee, and perhaps thou wouldst lose thy soul."

The old king said, "I know that if I should slay my son that I should shed innocent blood, for it is thou that hast sought to destroy him."

Having said this, Lamoni's father raised his sword to kill Ammon, but Ammon drew his own sword and fought with him. He withstood the king's blows, and then wounded him in the arm so that he could not fight any more. The king now had no way to defend himself, and saw that Ammon could kill him if he wished. So he began to plead for his life.

Ammon raised his sword and said, "I will smite thee except thou wilt grant unto me that my brethren may be cast out of prison."

The frightened king said, "If thou wilt spare me I will grant unto thee whatsoever thou wilt ask, even to half of the kingdom."

Ammon thought that the old king might harm Lamoni for having a Nephite with him, and even take away his throne. So while he had the king at his mercy he decided to make sure that Lamoni would also be protected.

He said, "If thou wilt grant that my brethren may be cast out of prison, and also that Lamoni may retain his kingdom, and that ye be not displeased with him, but grant that he may do according to his own desires in whatsoever thing he thinketh, then I will spare thee; otherwise I will smite thee to the earth."

This pleased the king. He was glad that his life would be spared, but he was happy also that Ammon loved Lamoni so much. He quickly granted Ammon's request, and even allowed Lamoni to be king in his own right. He said, "I will govern him no more."

The old king asked that he be taught more of the beliefs of Ammon, but Ammon and Lamoni had to hurry on to the land of Middoni.

122

Ammon pleads for his brothers . .

When they reached there, Lamoni went to the king, whose friend he was, and had the brethren of Ammon set free. The missionaries had suffered greatly. As they came out of prison, they had no clothes. They were both hungry and thirsty, and the ropes with which they were tied, had caused bad sores on their skin. Ammon was grieved because of their sufferings.

Although his brethren had been called upon to suffer so much at the hands of the wicked Lamanites who refused to listen to them, they were patient in it all. They knew they were enduring this persecution for the sake of the gospel, and therefore did not complain.

CHAPTER FORTY-THREE

Aaron's Sufferings

Alma 21.

*A*MMON'S brethren were fed and clothed when they were let out of prison. They had suffered much before Ammon's arrival, but they had been patient in their trouble, and had preached the gospel to many of the Lamanites, some of whom were converted.

This was Aaron's story:

When he left Ammon and his other brothers, Aaron went into a land where lived two groups of Lamanites, one known as Amalekites and the other the people of Amulon. They were named for their leaders.

These people were more wicked than the Lamanites to whom Ammon had gone, and they hated the Nephites.

When Aaron came to their city, he went to one of their synagogues which the Lamanites had built for their own religion, which was not of God. He began to preach to them, telling of his conversion to Christ.

One of the Lamanites rose up in the meeting and said, "What is that thou hast testified? Hast thou seen an angel? Why do not angels appear unto us? Behold are not this people as good as thy people? Thou sayest also, except we repent we shall perish. How knowest thou the thought and intent of our hearts? How knowest thou that we have cause to repent? How knowest thou that we are not a righteous people? We assemble ourselves together to worship God. We do believe that God will save all men."

Aaron asked this man if be believed that the Savior, Jesus, would come to redeem all men from their sins. The man said he did not believe any such thing. He called those teachings foolish traditions.

To prove that the Savior would come, Aaron opened the scriptures and read to them the prophecies about the coming of Christ, and of the resurrection. The people in the synagogue did not want to hear this doctrine, even though Aaron could prove it from the scriptures. They became angry as he continued to preach, and then mocked him.

When he saw how bitter they were, he left the synagogue, and walked out of the city, going to a small village nearby. There he found his two brethren preaching, but the people would not listen to them any more than the other group had listened to him.

Rejected by them all, the three missionary brethren went over into the land of Middoni where they again began to preach. A few people there believed, but most of them would not. Some became angry with them, and put them into prison. They took their clothes from them, and left them in their cells without either food or water. They tied them up so they could not escape.

After being freed by Ammon and Lamoni, they went out again, preaching in the synagogues of the city, and a great many people now began to believe their words.

CHAPTER FORTY-FOUR

Aaron Converts the King

Alma 21-22, 24.

Soon after Ammon had freed his brethren from prison in the land of Middoni, he and King Lamoni returned to their homes in the land of Ishmael where Lamoni reigned.

Lamoni commanded his servants to build synagogues in various parts of his kingdom, so that the people could meet together, and hear the gospel taught by Ammon. But Lamoni also preached to the people, and told them that now they were free from the rule of his father, the king of all the land. He told them they therefore had the right to worship the Lord according to their own desires, and that they need not fear that the old king would try to prevent them.

As Ammon and Lamoni left the land of Middoni to go to their homes, Aaron and his two companions also left, and went over to the land of Nephi, where the old king ruled.

They went directly to the palace and bowed low before the king. Aaron said, "Behold, O king, we are the brethren of Ammon whom thou hast delivered out of prison. And now, O king, if thou wilt spare our lives we will be thy servants."

The old king was pleased that the missionaries had come. He had been troubled in his mind ever since his meeting with Ammon. He knew that Ammon had no desire to kill him, as they had fought, and he desired to learn more of Ammon's teachings. Now that Ammon's brethren had come, he would have a chance to learn the truth.

He said, "I have been somewhat troubled in my mind because of the generosity and the greatness of the words of thy brother Ammon, and I desire to know the cause why he has not come up out of Middoni with thee."

127

Aaron explained, "Behold the Spirit of the Lord has called him another way. He has gone to the land of Ishmael to teach the people of Lamoni."

The king was even more interested and asked, "What is this that ye have said concerning the Spirit of the Lord? Behold this is the thing which doth trouble me. And also what is this that Ammon said, If ye will repent ye shall be saved, and if ye will not repent ye shall be cast off at the last day?"

Aaron asked him if he believed in God. The old king replied that he knew that some of his people believed there is a God, and that he had given them the right to worship. Then he added, "And if now thou sayest there is a God, behold I will believe."

He asked Aaron if God was the Great Spirit who had brought his forefathers out of Jerusalem. Aaron told him that he was, and that the Great Spirit is God. He then began to preach the gospel to the old king.

After listening carefully, the old king knelt down and began to pray, saying, "O God, Aaron hath told me that there is a God; and if there is a God, and if thou art God, wilt thou make thyself known unto me and I will give away all my sins to know thee, and that I may be raised from the dead and be saved at the last day?"

When he had said this, he fell to the earth as though he were dead. The Lord's spirit had overcome him, as it had overcome his son Lamoni.

The king's servants ran to the queen and told her what had happened, and she hurried to where the king lay. She saw Aaron and his brethren standing there, and thought they had struck him down. She called her servants and commanded them to arrest the missionaries, and slay them. But the servants had seen what had happened, and they knew that Aaron and his brothers had not struck the king. They were afraid to lay hands on them, and began to plead with the queen, saying, "Why commandest thou that we should slay these men, when behold one of them is mightier than us all? Therefore we shall fall before them."

When the queen saw how frightened her servants were, she became afraid also, thinking that some evil power had come into the house. She ordered her servants to call in the people of the city, that they might slay Aaron and his brothers, if the servants were afraid.

Aaron knew that if a large crowd came into the palace and saw the king lying there, and heard the queen accuse the missionaries of bringing evil into the house, there would be trouble among the people. He did not want this, so he went over to where the king lay, and touched him on the shoulder, saying, "Stand."

Strength came back to the king, and he stood up. Seeing this, the queen and all her servants were stricken with fear. But the king began to talk with them, and preached so sincerely that his whole household was converted to the Lord.

Hearing of the miracle in the palace, many of the people assembled there. When they saw the Nephite missionaries, they began to murmur against them, but the king told them the truth about Aaron and his brothers. He asked the missionaries to stand in front of the crowd, and invited them to speak to the people.

The king then issued a proclamation to all the people in his kingdom, saying that no one could harm Ammon, or Aaron and their brothers, as they preached the gospel. Thousands were converted by the missionaries after this, and all who were converted laid down their weapons of war and did not fight any more.

There were still many Lamanites who were not converted, and who continued in their evil ways. Those who had joined the Church now wished to be separated from these wicked ones, and have a different name. After talking with Aaron and his brethren about it, the king decided to call all the converted Lamanites, Anti-Nephi-Lehi.

CHAPTER FORTY-FIVE

A Lamanite Rebellion

Alma 24.

ONE GROUP of Lamanites known as Amalekites were among the most wicked of them all. They hated the Nephites very bitterly. When they learned of the missionary labors of the sons of Mosiah, and that so many of the Lamanites were converted to their teachings, the Amalekites became very angry. They felt that the converted Lamanites had become traitors, and had gone over to the side of the Nephites.

Because of this, the Amalekites went among other Lamanites and began to stir them up against the converted Lamanites who had taken the name of Anti-Nephi-Lehi. They were also very bitter against the old king, who had himself been converted, saying that he was no longer fit to be king, and urging the people to start a rebellion against him.

The king was in failing health, and believed it would be wise to turn the kingdom over to one of his sons, which he did. Within a year the old king died.

When Ammon and his brothers heard of the rebellion, they hurried to the land of Ishmael, where a meeting was held by the believing Lamanites to discuss plans for their defense if they were attacked. But these people did not wish to fight.

King Lamoni stood before them and told them of their former sins, and reminded them that the Lord had been gracious in forgiving them. Now, he said, if they stained their swords with human blood once more, the Lord might not forgive them this time. He told his people it would be better for them to bury their weapons in the ground, and even be killed themselves, rather than to shed blood again.

He said, "And now, my brethren, if our brethren seek to destroy us, behold we will hide away our swords, yea even we will bury them deep in the earth that they may be kept bright as a testimony that we have never used them, at the last day; and if our brethren destroy us behold we shall go to our God and shall be saved."

Hearing this, the people dug holes in the earth and buried all their swords and other weapons of war. They did this as a testimony to the Lord and to all men that they would never again shed human blood.

The wicked Lamanites sent their army against the people of Anti-Nephi-Lehi. As they saw the army coming, the righteous Lamanites, now without any weapons, walked out to meet them. They did not raise an arm to defend themselves.

The army began to slay them, and killed more than a thousand. But when they saw that these people did not even defend themselves, they stopped the terrible slaughter. Many of the enemy soldiers, seeing the faith of the believing Lamanites, became converted themselves, and joined the people of God. More were converted that day than were killed in the attack.

The soldiers who were converted threw down their own weapons and they too made a covenant that they would never fight again.

Although the rest of the army, which was not converted, did no longer kill the converted Lamanites, they still were angry at the Nephites, and planned to make war against them. They marched against the city of Zarahemla. But the Nephites were stronger than they were, and drove the Lamanite army back with heavy losses.

When the Lamanites saw that they could not defeat the Nephites, they returned to their own land. Some of them believed that the power of the Lord was with the Nephites, and they came over and joined the converted Lamanites, known as the people of Anti-

Nephi-Lehi. They also buried their weapons and promised never to go to war again.

The people of Anti-Nephi-Lehi now wished to join the Nephites and worship the Lord with them. Ammon went to the Lord in prayer, to ask if this was his will. The Lord told him that he must move his followers to Zarahemla, or they would be killed by the wicked Lamanites.

Ammon took them to Zarahemla. There they were welcomed by the Nephites who gave them the land of Jershon, near to Zarahemla, for their homes. They became known among the Nephites as the people of Ammon.

When the Nephites learned that the people of Ammon would rather die than go to war, they stationed an army near the land of Jershon to protect them.

CHAPTER FORTY-SIX

Nehor the False Prophet

Alma 1.

*I*N THE DAYS when Alma was chief judge and governor in Zarahemla, a man named Nehor came among the people, preaching false doctrines.

He told them that it did not matter if they sinned, for they would be saved in the kingdom of God anyway. He said also that the officers of the Church should not have to work to support themselves, as they did among the Nephites, but that the preachers should live upon the contributions of the people.

Because some of the Nephites loved sin, it pleased them to think that they could be saved no matter what they did, so they followed Nehor. As they gave him money for preaching, he bought fine clothes. So many believed him that he organized a church of his own.

One day as he walked through the city, he met Gideon, who had helped bring the people of King Limhi out of slavery among the Lamanites. Gideon was now an old man, but he was faithful in the true Church of God.

Nehor began teaching his untrue ideas to Gideon, but Gideon knew the scriptures well, and was able to prove that Nehor was wrong. This made Nehor angry, and he drew his sword and killed the old man.

The people seized Nehor, and took him before Alma the judge. There he began to preach his false doctrines to Alma and tried to justify himself in his crime.

Alma listened to him, but then said that he was guilty of murder. He also told him that it was wrong to accept money for preaching. This he called priestcraft. He condemned Nehor for both sins, killing the aged Gideon, and preaching for money.

133

Nehor was taken to a high hill in Zarahemla. There he confessed his sins. After he had done so, he was executed by the officers of the law.

His death did not end his teachings. The apostate church still lasted, and its leaders continued to preach for money. They caused a division among the people of Zarahemla. The true Saints of God were persecuted by the followers of Nehor and other wicked people.

The officers of the true Church continued to preach the gospel, and also worked for their own living. In spite of the persecution that came upon them, the Saints served the Lord, and he blessed them.

CHAPTER FORTY-SEVEN

A Rebel Seeks To Be King

Alma 2-3.

AMLICI, one of the followers of the wicked Nehor, aspired to be king of the Nephites. It had been five years since Mosiah, the former king, had told the people to govern themselves without kings.

But Amlici believed the teachings of Nehor, and wished to destroy the Church of God. He thought that if he became king, he could prevent the Saints from worshipping the Lord.

He went among the people, teaching that they should have a king instead of being ruled by Alma and the other judges. Many foolish ones believed him, and they were willing to make him king. But the law of the land required that any change in the government must be made through an election, with the majority of the people voting for the change.

An election was held, and Amlici was defeated. Disappointed, he gathered his own followers about him, and set himself up as king over them. Then he ordered them to arm themselves and start a civil war. He thought that through such a war, he could overthrow the government even though he had lost the election.

By this time, thousands of people had accepted his leadership. They joined the army he was raising, and prepared to fight against Alma and the rest of the people.

When Alma learned what Amlici was doing, he armed his own men. Amlici and his soldiers encamped on a hill near the river Sidon, which flowed past the city of Zarahemla. There Alma's army attacked them. Both forces fought hard. The Lord blessed Alma's men, and gave them great strength. With his help,

135

they beat back the followers of Amlici, who turned and ran for their lives.

Alma's soldiers gave chase and killed many of them. When evening came, they camped. During the night, Alma sent our four spies to see which way the Amlicites were going, and try to learn their plans.

The spies came back in great fear, and told Alma that the Amlicites had joined an army of the Lamanites, and had marched against the city of Minon, north of Zarahemla, where they were killing the people. It was the intention of the Lamanites and Amlicites to march against Zarahemla and seize the city. Amlici still wanted to be king.

Alma took his soldiers back toward Zarahemla to defend the city. As they reached the banks of the river Sidon, they met the combined armies of Amlicites and Lamanites.

Both sides lost thousands of men. During the battle, Alma met Amlici face to face and they began to fight. Amlici was a powerful man and a good fighter. Alma knew this. He prayed to the Lord for help and Amlici was killed.

Shortly after this, Alma met the king of the Lamanites, who also fought with him. The king was rescued by his guards, who came out against Alma. But Alma's guards protected him.

When the Amlicites joined the Lamanite army, they painted their faces like the Lamanites, to frighten the Nephites. But the Nephites were not afraid. They fought in the strength of the Lord, and although they were fewer in number than the Lamanites and the Amlicites, they won the battle, and drove their enemies out of the land.

The many dead were thrown into the river Sidon, and their bodies drifted out to sea.

CHAPTER FORTY-EIGHT

Alma the Missionary

Alma 8.

ALMA, the chief judge and governor of the land of Zarahemla, was also the leader of the Church. Among the people there were Nephites who were not members of the Church, and others who had been members, but had fallen into sin.

Alma desired to take a missionary journey among them. But he disliked to neglect his work as governor. He knew that it was more important for him to preach to the people and convert them than it was for him to be governor, so he resigned this position and Nephihah was appointed in his place.

Alma went from city to city teaching the people the gospel, and calling them to repentance. Many followed his advice, and turned to the Lord.

There was one very wicked city called Ammonihah, where Satan had great power. Alma hoped that he could turn these people from their evil ways, and bring them into the Church.

He prayed earnestly to the Lord to guide and help him in his mission to this city. But though he worked hard, and sought the aid of the Lord, the people there would not listen to him.

They said, "We know that thou art Alma, and we know that thou art the high priest over the Church which thou hast established in many parts of the land, according to your tradition; and we are not of thy Church, and we do not believe in such foolish traditions. And now we know that because we are not of thy Church that thou hast no power over us; and thou hast delivered up the judgment seat unto Nephihah, therefore thou art not chief judge over us."

They abused him, and spit at him, and cast him out of their city.

Sorrowfully, he walked toward the city of Aaron. He was grieved by the sinfulness of the people of Ammonihah, knowing what judgments would come upon them if they did not repent. But they had rejected him and his message.

On the road, an angel of the Lord appeared to him, and comforted him. It was the same angel who had appeared to Alma and the sons of Mosiah when, as young men, they had gone about fighting the Church. He said, "I am sent to command thee that thou return to the city of Ammonihah and preach again unto the people of that city; yea, preach unto them, yea, say unto them, except they repent the Lord God will destroy them. For behold they do study at this time that they may destroy the liberty of thy people."

When Alma received this message, he turned about, and hurried back. He entered the city by a different road from the one he had taken before. He had been fasting, and was tired and hungry. Going up to a certain man, he said, "Will ye give to an humble servant of God something to eat?"

The man said, "I am a Nephite, and I know that thou art a holy prophet of God, for thou art the man whom an angel said in a vision, Thou shalt receive. Therefore, go with me into my house, and I will impart unto thee of my food, and I know that thou wilt be a blessing unto me and my house."

This man was named Amulek. The Lord had sent the angel to visit him, also, commanding him to take care of Alma.

When Alma and Amulek reached the house, Amulek brought the prophet bread and meat. Alma was refreshed, and offered a prayer to the Lord thanking him for his blessings. He also blessed Amulek for his kindness to him.

After dinner the prophet turned to Amulek and said, "I am Alma, and am the high priest over the Church of God throughout the land. And behold I have been called to preach the word of God among all this people according to the spirit of revelation and prophecy; and I was in this land and they would not receive me, but they cast me out and I was about to set my back towards this land forever. But behold, I have been commanded that I should turn again and prophesy unto this people, yea, and to testify against them concerning their iniquities. And now, Amulek, because thou hast fed me and taken me in, thou art blessed, for I was an hungered, for I had fasted many days."

Alma lived for some time in the house of Amulek resting, and preparing to preach to the wicked people of the city.

CHAPTER FORTY-NINE

A Wicked Lawyer Converted

Alma 8-15.

*T*HE LORD spoke to Alma, commanding him to begin his work in the city of Ammonihah. He also called Amulek to assist Alma. The two men went among the unbelieving people, preaching the gospel to them. The Lord gave them great power, and he protected their lives when the wicked tried to slay them.

Amulek was a great help to Alma in this work. He told the people he knew Alma was a true prophet, for an angel of the Lord had come to him and told him about Alma, and instructed him to meet the prophet and take him into his house and feed him.

Some of the lawyers of the city argued with the two missionaries, asking them questions, and trying to confuse them. But Alma and Amulek resisted them and embarrassed them before the people. This made the lawyers angry, and they tried in every way to show that the missionaries had broken a law, and should be put in prison.

One of the most expert among these lawyers was Zeezrom, and he led the others in questioning Alma and Amulek. He lied to the missionaries, and tried to twist what they said so that it did not mean what was intended. But Amulek, being filled with the spirit, confounded Zeezrom, showing him how wrong he was.

So forcefully did Alma and Amulek speak, and so well did they confound the wicked lawyers, that many of the people who had listened began to believe their teachings. But most of the people grew more and more angry with the two missionaries. At last, in their rage, they seized Alma and Amulek, bound them with strong ropes, and took them before their chief judge. There they made lying accusations against them, seeking to have them put in prison or killed.

140

Zeezrom, the lawyer who had been confounded by Amulek, heard the false charges. As he listened to the lies being told about the two missionaries, and seeing how unjust his neighbors were, he began to repent, realizing that what Alma and Amulek had said was right. He was troubled about his own sins, knowing that he had caused the people to believe falsehoods such as they were now telling to the judge. His conscience hurt him sorely.

He spoke to the people who were assembled, and said, "I am guilty, and these men are spotless before God."

Zeezrom pleaded for the lives of Alma and Amulek, and defended them. Instead of doing as he asked, the people turned against him, and spit on him. They asked him if he had become possessed of the devil, and then cast him out, and sent men after him to stone him to death.

Filled with rage, the wicked men then sought for all those who had believed the teachings of Alma and Amulek, and brought in as many as they could find. These people, men, women and little children, were tied up before Alma and Amulek. Then all their books including the scriptures, were brought together and burned. When the fire was hot, these believers were thrown into it.

Alma and Amulek were then shown the suffering of their followers who were being burned to death. When Amulek saw it, he was broken hearted, and said to Alma, "How can we witness this awful scene? Therefore let us stretch forth our hands, and exercise the power of God and save them from the flames."

But Alma said, "The Spirit constraineth me that I must not stretch forth mine hand; for behold the Lord receiveth them up unto himself in glory; and he doth suffer that they may do this thing, or that the people may do this thing unto them, according to the hardness of their hearts, that the judgments which he shall exercise upon them in his wrath may be just. And the blood of the innocent shall stand as a witness against them."

Fearful himself, Amulek now said, "Perhaps they will burn us also."

But Alma knew the will of the Lord. He comforted Amulek and said, "Our work is not finished; therefore they will burn us not."

When the fires died down, and the innocent people were dead, and their scriptures consumed, the chief judge of the city came to Alma and Amulek, as they stood bound, struck them in the face, and said, "After what ye have seen will ye preach again unto this people, that they shall be cast into a lake of fire and brimstone? Ye see that ye had no power to save those who had been cast into the fire; neither has God saved them because they were of thy faith."

He struck their faces again, and asked, "What say ye for yourselves?"

This judge belonged to the church which had been started by the apostate Nehor, who killed Gideon.

Neither Alma nor Amulek replied to the judge. Angered still more when they refused to speak, he slapped them again, and had them put in prison.

Three days later, more lawyers and judges, all members of the church of Nehor, came to the prison and questioned the missionaries but still they remained silent.

The chief judge stood before them and said, "Why do ye not answer the words of this people? Know ye not that I have power to deliver you up unto the flames?" They still said nothing.

The next day the judge and the lawyers came back, and once more questioned them, and when the missionaries refused to speak, the evil men spit on them. For days afterward, they came back to the prison and mocked the missionaries. Alma and Amulek were given nothing to eat and no water to drink during this time. Their enemies took their clothing from them also, and left them bound inside the prison.

Then the chief judge came again, bringing with him many of the lawyers and teachers of the city. He struck them many times and said, "If ye have the power of God, deliver yourselves from these bands, and then we will believe that the Lord will destroy this people according to your words."

All who were with the judge then came up and struck the two prisoners, repeating what he had said. When the last one had struck them, and reviled them, Alma and Amulek arose to their feet, and cried out, "How long shall we suffer these great afflictions, O Lord? Give us the strength according to our faith which is in Christ, even unto deliverance."

Given great power from heaven, they broke the cords which held them bound. When the judge and his companions saw this, they became frightened, and ran for their lives. They feared that destruction would come upon them.

Before they reached the door, an earthquake shook down the prison, killing the judge and all his wicked companions. Alma and Amulek were not hurt.

The collapse of the prison made a great noise, which was heard by the people of the city. Many came running to see what had happened. When they saw Alma and Amulek walking away from the ruins of the prison, they became frightened also, and ran away.

The Lord now commanded his two servants to leave the city and go to the land of Sidom. There they found some of the people who had been converted in the wicked city of Ammonihah. They had been cast out of the city and stoned, but had escaped with their lives.

Among them was Zeezrom, the lawyer who had repented. He was sick with a fever. When he heard that Alma and Amulek were in the city, he sent for them, and they came and visited him. He asked them to heal him by the power of the Lord.

143

Alma took his hand and said, "Believest thou in the power of Christ unto salvation?"

Zeezrom answered, "Yea, I believe all the words that thou hast taught."

Alma then prayed to the Lord to heal Zeezrom. Immediately the repentant lawyer arose from his sick bed, perfectly well. Alma took him out and baptized him into the Church. Zeezrom then became a missionary for the Church, and preached the gospel to all who would listen to him.

The healing of Zeezrom . .

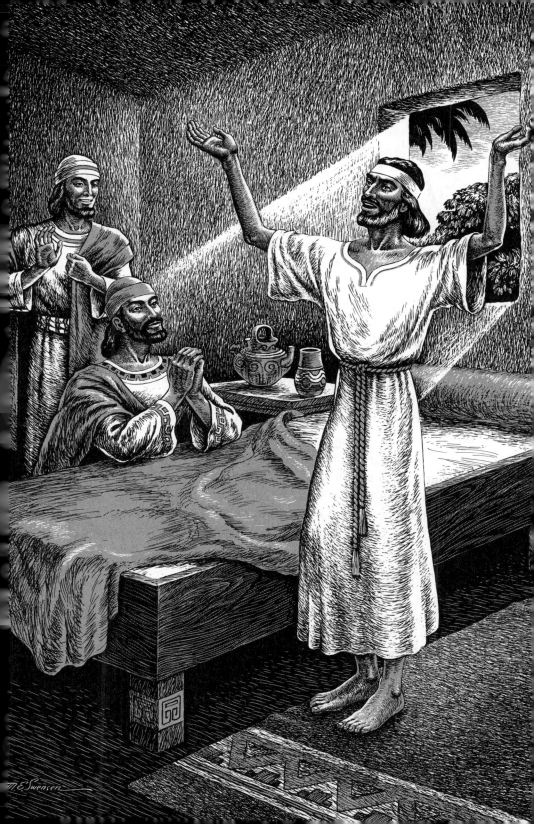

CHAPTER FIFTY

The Wicked City Destroyed

Alma 16.

*T*HE PEOPLE in the city of Ammonihah had boasted that they could not be destroyed. They had laughed at Alma and Amulek when they warned them. They did not believe in the Lord, and persecuted his servants.

Soon after Alma and Amulek had gone, the Lamanites began once more to make war against the Nephites. They moved so fast that they conquered several cities before the Nephites could raise an army to stop them.

Directly in the path of the invading Lamanites lay the wicked city of Ammonihah. The people there were not strong enough to resist such a force. The Lamanites came into the city and in one day killed every person in it, and destroyed their homes and other buildings.

The Lamanites left without burying any of the dead. Only dogs and wild animals were left to roam the streets. The smell from the dead was so bad that the Nephites came and gathered together all the bodies, and covered them with dirt.

From that time on, the land of Ammonihah became known as the Desolation of Nehors. All of those who were killed were members of the apostate church of Nehor.

The Nephite armies now came against their enemies. But the Lamanites had already captured several cities and taken many prisoners. One Nephite army set out to find the prisoners and rescue them. They came upon the Lamanite army which was guarding them. The Lamanites scattered, and ran for their lives, leaving all the prisoners behind. The Nephite army then returned the prisoners to Zarahemla.

Alma and Amulek continued their preaching in various parts of the land, and many people repented of their sins, and turned to the Lord.

Zeezrom assisted them from time to time. Many people had been surprised at his conversion, and were more surprised when he was healed of his sickness. He became a loyal worker in the Church.

Once more the Church was established in all parts of the land, and the spirit of apostasy was overcome. There were no iniquities among the people, and the Lord poured out his spirit upon all; the hearts of all people were softened.

Priests and teachers were called to assist in the work, and they taught the people to avoid lying, stealing, robbing, and the many other things which had caused so much distress among the people before they began to repent.

CHAPTER FIFTY-ONE

Korihor the Anti-Christ

Alma 30.

*I*N THE LAND of Zarahemla lived a man named Korihor. He was a good speaker, but he had very little faith in God.

One day Satan appeared to him like an angel of light. Satan is a real person. He does not have a body of flesh and bones as we do, but he does have a body of spirit just like our spirits before we came to the earth to live.

It was this same Satan who tempted Adam and Eve in the Garden of Eden. It was he also who long ago had come to Moses, trying to deceive him, saying that he was the Savior. Moses rebuked him and drove him away.

But when Satan came to Korihor, the Nephite listened to what he said. The devil wanted to deceive Korihor, as well as all of the other Nephites.

Satan told Korihor to go among the Nephites, preaching to them that there is no God, and that they could sin and live any way they liked, for, he said, death ends everything.

Doing as Satan told him, Korihor went among the people teaching these things. He said, "Why do ye yoke yourselves with such foolish things? Why do ye look for a Christ? For no man can know of anything which is to come. * * *Ye cannot know of things which ye do not see, therefore ye cannot know that there shall be a Christ."

He told them many other things which were not true. Some of the foolish Nephites believed what Korihor said, and were led into sin.

He went over into the land of Jershon where the people of Ammon lived. They were wiser than the Nephites, and when Korihor tried to teach them evil ways, they caught him, tied him up, and brought him before Ammon, who was the high priest in that part of the land. He told his followers to put Korihor out of their city.

Korihor then went to the land of Gideon, and preached there, but those people also saw that he was evil, and would not listen to him. They bound him and took him before their high priest and their governor.

The high priest asked Korihor, "Why do ye go about perverting the ways of the Lord? Why do ye teach people that there shall be no Christ? Why do ye speak against all the prophecies of the holy prophets?"

Korihor called the prophecies foolish traditions, and told the people they could not prove they were true. He accused the high priest of leading the people astray, and placing them in bondage.

When the governor and the high priest saw how bitter Korihor was, they refused to argue with him. They left him bound with cords, and had him taken back to Zarahemla to appear before the governor there, and also before Alma the high priest.

When he stood before them, Korihor began to blaspheme. He reviled the priests and teachers of the Church, and accused them of taxing the people and living in luxury upon the money.

Alma stopped him, and said, "Thou knowest that we do not glut ourselves upon the labors of this people; for behold I have labored even from the commencement of the reign of the judges until now, with mine own hands for my support, notwithstanding my many travels round about the land to declare the word of God, unto my people. And notwithstanding the many labors which I have performed in the Church, I have never received so much as even one senine (Nephite money) for my labor."

Alma told the wicked Korihor that none of the officers of the Church preached for money, and their only reward was the joy of doing the work of the Lord.

"Then why sayest thou that we preach unto this people to get gain," Alma continued, "when thou, of thyself, knowest that we receive no gain?"

Alma asked Korihor if he thought the brethren were deceiving the people, and Korihor said he did.

Then Alma said, "Believest thou that there is a God?"

And he answered, "Nay."

Now Alma said, "Will ye deny again that there is a God, and also deny the Christ? For behold I say unto you, I know there is a God, and also that Christ shall come."

Remembering that Korihor had said there was no evidence to prove the gospel is true, Alma asked, "And now what evidence have ye that there is no God, or that Christ cometh not? I say unto you that ye have none, save it be your word only. But behold, I have all things as a testimony that these things are true, and ye also have all things as a testimony unto you that they are true, and will ye deny them? Believest thou that these things are true?"

Alma knew that Korihor believed in God, even though he was doing what Satan told him to do, and he said to the wicked man, "I know that thou believest, but thou art possessed with a lying spirit, and ye have put off the spirit of God that it may have no place in you; but the devil has power over you, and he doth carry you about, working devices that he may destroy the children of God."

Korihor now said to Alma, "If thou wilt show me a sign, that I may be convinced that there is a God, yea, show unto me that he hath power, then will I be convinced of the truth of thy words."

The Savior once said that a person is wicked, when he asks for a sign. Alma knew this, and said, "Thou hast had signs enough; will ye tempt your God? Will ye say, Show me a sign, when ye have the testimony of all those thy brethren and also all the holy prophets?"

Then Alma showed him how the scriptures prove that there is a God, and that the Lord created the earth and everything on it. "And yet," Alma said, "do ye go about leading away the hearts of this people, testifying unto them there is no God? And yet will ye deny against all these witnesses?"

Korihor replied, "Yes, I will deny except ye shall show me a sign."

Alma was grieved in his soul for Korihor. Yet he knew that if Korihor were allowed to continue preaching, he would lead many others to sin, and then not only would Korihor's soul be lost, but also all those who believed his false teachings.

Alma was patient. He desired Korihor to repent. But Korihor continued to ask for a sign.

Alma said, "If thou shalt deny again, behold God shall smite thee that thou shalt become dumb, that thou shalt never open thy mouth any more, that thou shalt not deceive this people any more."

Korihor was stubborn, and still resisted Alma, again denying God.

At last Alma said, "This will I give unto thee for a sign, that thou shalt be struck dumb according to my words; and I say that in the name of God ye shall be struck dumb that ye shall no more have utterance."

At once the Lord struck Korihor dumb. He could not say a word.

When the governor saw what had happened, he wrote a letter to Korihor and asked, "Art thou convinced of the power of God? In whom did ye desire that Alma should show forth his sign? Would ye that he should afflict others, to show unto thee a sign? Behold, he has showed unto you a sign; and now will ye dispute more?"

Korihor wrote back to the governor saying, "I know that I am dumb, for I cannot speak, and I know that nothing, save it were the power of God, could bring this upon me; yea and I also knew that there was a God."

He then told Alma and the governor that the devil had come to him as an angel of light, and had commanded him to preach these false doctrines. Then he asked Alma to take the curse away, so that he could speak again. But Alma said, "If this curse should be taken from thee, thou wouldst again lead away the hearts of this people; therefore, it shall be unto thee, even as the Lord will."

The Lord did not remove the curse. Korihor, now unable to say a word, was cast out of the city, and went from house to house begging for food. One day, while walking in the street he was run over and killed.

Alma published a proclamation to all the people telling them what had happened to Korihor. Those who had believed in the teachings of the wicked preacher, now were able to see that they were mistaken in following him. They repented, and came back to the true Church of God.

CHAPTER FIFTY-TWO

Alma Teaches Prayer

Alma 34.

ALMA was a great preacher. He was a true prophet, inspired of the Lord as were Moses, Elijah and other chosen men of God.

One of his greatest sermons was on prayer. He taught the people to pray to the Lord in all they did, that he might help and guide them, prosper them in their work, and increase their faith. He said:

"Yea, cry unto him for mercy, for he is mighty to save.

"Yea, humble yourselves, and continue in prayer unto him.

"Cry unto him when ye are in your fields, yea over all your flocks.

"Cry unto him in your houses, yea over all your household, both morning, mid-day, and evening.

"Yea, cry unto him against the power of your enemies.

"Yea, cry unto him against the devil, who is an enemy to all righteousness.

"Cry unto him over the crops of your fields, that ye may prosper in them.

"Cry over the flocks of your fields, that they may increase.

"But this is not all; ye must pour our your souls in your closets, and in your secret places, and in your wilderness.

"Yea, and when you do not cry unto the Lord, let your hearts be full, drawn out in prayer unto him continually for your welfare, and also for the welfare of those who are around you."

Alma himself knew the power of prayer, and also of fasting. The Lord gave to him many revelations as a result of his prayers and righteous living, and sent angels to help him in his work.

But Alma taught also that we must be kind to others. He told the people that neither prayer nor faith alone is enough. We must have works with our faith and prayers. We must live the gospel, and be kind to all people. So after he had taught them to pray for their blessings, he said, "Now behold, my beloved brethren, I say unto you, do not suppose that this is all. For after ye have done all these things, if ye turn away the needy, and the naked, and visit not the sick and afflicted, and impart of your substance, if ye have, to those who stand in need—I say unto you, if ye do not any of these things, behold your prayer is vain, and availeth you nothing, and ye are as hypocrites who do deny the faith.

"Therefore, if ye do not remember to be charitable, ye are as dross, which the refiners do cast out (it being of no worth) and is trodden under foot of men."

CHAPTER FIFTY-THREE

Alma and His Sons

Alma 36 to 42.

*A*LMA took some of the faithful brethren, and two of his own sons, and began a mission among the Zoramites.

The Zoramites were a wicked people who had rejected the true gospel, and formed a church of their own. They dressed in fine clothes, and wore many ornaments. Their priests were among the rich men of the land, and obtained their wealth from the people. The poor were oppressed.

Alma and his brethren were successful in converting some of these people, but most of them would not listen to what they said, so the missionaries left them to labor in another place.

The leaders of the Zoramites wished to know which of the people had accepted the teachings of Alma, and when they found out, they drove the believers out of the land.

Forced from their homes, these people travelled in the wilderness until they came to the land of Jershon, where the people of Ammon lived. There they were received with kindness, and were fed and clothed.

When the Zoramites learned of this, they were very angry, and wanted to fight the Nephites and the people of Ammon for being so kind to those whom they had driven away.

Alma heard of it, and helped prepare for this new war. Before it began, however, he talked with his sons. He did not know how long he would be permitted to live, and he wished to prepare them for the future.

He called the boys in, one by one, first talking with Helaman, a splendid young man. To Helaman he gave the sacred records, and told him to continue to write upon them. Helaman was faithful to the Lord, which Alma knew, but Alma wished to bear his testimony to him. He told of his own conversion when the angel of the Lord stopped him and the sons of Mosiah in their evil way, and he taught him that Jesus would come as the Christ, the Savior of the world. He asked Helaman to preach the gospel to the people, just as Alma had, and urged him to live close to the Lord, drawing near to him in prayer. He said:

"O remember, my son, and learn wisdom in thy youth; yea, learn in thy youth to keep the commandments of God. Yea, cry unto God for all thy support; yea, let all thy doings be unto the Lord, and whithersoever thou goest, let it be in the Lord, yea, let thy thoughts be directed unto the Lord; yea, let the affections of thy heart be placed upon the Lord forever."

Another of the beautiful sayings of Alma was:

"Counsel with the Lord in all thy doings, and he will direct thee for good; yea, when thou liest down at night, lie down unto the Lord, that he may watch over you in your sleep; and when thou risest in the morning let thy heart be full of thanks unto God; and if ye do these things, ye shall be lifted up at the last day."

Alma gave Helaman the ball, or director, which the Lord had given to Lehi in addition to the plates. They called the director the Liahona, which being interpreted, means a compass. In doing so, he said:

"Just as surely as this director did bring our fathers by following its course, to the promised land, shall the words of Christ, if we follow their course, carry us beyond this vale of sorrow into a far better land of promise."

He bade farewell to his son by saying, "And now my son, see that ye take care of these sacred things; yea, see that ye look to God and live. Go unto this people, and declare the word, and be sober. My son, farewell."

He next called his son Shiblon to him, and counselled him to be faithful, and to control himself, and be meek, never giving way to anger.

Then he called to him his erring son Corianton, who was a wicked young man. Corianton had committed many evil deeds, and had even lost his virtue. Alma called him to repentance and told him that sex sin is more abominable than any other sin except murder and the sin against the Holy Ghost. He said, "I would to God that ye had not been guilty of so great a crime. I would not dwell upon your crimes, to harrow up your soul, if it were not for your good. But behold, ye cannot hide your crimes from God, and except ye repent, they will stand as a testimony against you at the last day."

He told Corianton to take the advice of his older brothers, and no longer allow himself to be led into temptation by evil companions.

Alma then taught his son about Jesus, who would come as the Savior of the world. He told him of the great atonement of the Lord, and explained that we would not only live in this world, but also after our bodies die. The spirits of the righteous dead go to Paradise, a place of departed spirits, where there is happiness, peace and joy, and they remain there until the resurrection. But he said, the spirits of the wicked go to a prison house where they are punished for their sins. At the resurrection, the righteous are taken into the presence of God, but the wicked are kept out, because they are unclean.

He told Corianton that our mortal life is a time in which the Lord expects us to overcome our weaknesses, and become clean and strong in the faith, loyal to God, keeping his commandments. If we live right we will escape the punishments which come to the wicked. He explained that if we do sin in this life, and sincerely repent, and commit those sins no more, and keep the commandments, the Lord will forgive us, and accept us into his kingdom. In his farewell, he asked his son to become worthy to go on a mission and preach the gospel to the people.

CHAPTER FIFTY-FOUR

The Zoramite War

Alma 43 and 44.

THE ZORAMITES wanted to start a war with the Nephites. When they had driven out of their land the people who had been converted by Alma and his fellow missionaries, the Zoramites had hoped that these converts would die in the wilderness. But they went over to the land of Jershon where the people of Ammon lived among the Nephites, and there they were treated kindly. It was because of this that the Zoramites desired to wage war against the Nephites.

The Zoramites hated righteousness. They hated God, and they hated the Nephites because they had taught his gospel among the Zoramite people. The Zoramite church paid its preachers well for teaching their false doctrines. The Nephite priests and teachers worked for their living, and taught the Zoramties that all true servants of God should do the same. This angered the Zoramite priests who said their "craft was in danger." They stirred up the people against the Nephites.

Feeling they needed larger armies than they themselves had, the Zoramites asked the Lamanites to join them in attacking the Nephites. The Lamanites agreed and together they prepared for war.

The leading general among the Nephites was a righteous man named Moroni. It was not the Moroni who gave the plates to Joseph Smith, but a man who lived about five hundred years earlier than the son of Mormon.

The combined Lamanite and Zoramite armies were twice as large as his own, so Moroni knew that he would have to find some new way to protect his men.

The soldiers in those days used swords, spears, and bows and arrows. They fought hand to hand without armor of any kind, having no protection except the weapons they carried.

Moroni decided to put armor on his men. He made breast-plates to protect their bodies and armored sleeves or arm shields, so that their arms would not be injured easily. He also made heavy helmets for their heads. He dressed his men in heavy clothing too, which was a protection to them.

He had trenches dug around the cities of the Nephites, with dirt embankments in front to further protect his men who could fight from behind these earth-works, shooting arrows and sling-ing stones at their enemy from a distance.

Moroni was only twenty-five years old when he became com-mander-in-chief of all the Nephite armies, but even though he was a young man, he was so skilled in warfare that the Nephites were glad to follow him.

The commander of the combined Zoramite and Lamanite armies was named Zerahemnah. He marched his men against the Nephites, but when he saw how well armed and protected they were, he was afraid to attack because his own men were entirely naked except for a small cloth about their hips. Therefore he called his soldiers back into the wilderness. He planned to march against some other Nephite city, thinking that Moroni had not fortified the more distant places.

Moroni sent out spies to watch the movement of the enemy. He also went to Alma the prophet, asking him to inquire of the Lord if they should follow and attack the Lamanites.

The Lord through Alma told Moroni that the Lamanites were going toward the city of Manti. He also said that the Nephites were to defend their homes and families, even to bloodshed if necessary.

Leaving part of his army to protect Zarahemla, Moroni and the rest went quickly to Manti. He sent word to the people who lived there to prepare to fight because the Lamanites were on their way to attack them. The people of Manti prepared. Then Moroni took his men into hiding in a valley by the River Sidon. He placed spies all about to tell him when the Lamanite army approached the city.

The spies returned and told him the enemy was moving toward the valley. Moroni divided his army so that he could attack from two sides.

As the Lamanites marched into the valley, one-half of the Nephite army, commanded by a man named Lehi, marched in behind them, and attacked from the rear. The Lamanites turned to fight them, when the second half of Moroni's army came out of hiding, and attacked from the other side.

The Nephites were protected by their armor, and thousands of the Lamanites were killed. Seeing they were being defeated, the Lamanites retreatd but the Nephites followed closely.

Knowing they might be destroyed, the Lamanites now fought harder than they had ever done. So fierce was their attack that many of the Nephite soldiers became frightened and wished to break from their ranks and run. Seeing this, Moroni came among them, telling them that every one of them would be slaves to the Lamanites if they and their families were captured.

The Nephites began to pray for the help of God, that they might remain free, and be allowed to worship the Lord as they desired.

The Lord answered their prayers and strengthened their arms. They drove the Lamanites into one section of the valley, and completely surrounded them. When the Lamanites saw they were trapped they were terrified.

Seeing their fright, Moroni commanded his men to stop fighting. Then he asked the enemy general Zerahemnah to surrender. He said, "Ye know that we do not desire to be men of blood. Ye know that ye are in our hands, yet we do not desire to slay you. Behold, we have not come out to battle against you, that we might shed your blood for power; neither do we desire to bring any one to the yoke of bondage. But this is the very cause for which ye have come against us; yea, and ye are angry with us because of our religion."

He told Zerahemna that it was through the blessing of the Lord that the Nephites had fought with such strength that day. Then he said, "I command you, by all the desires which ye have for life, that ye deliver up your weapons of war unto us, and we will seek not your blood, but we will spare your lives, if ye will go your way, and come not again to war against us. And now, if ye do not this, behold, ye are in our hands, and I will command my men that they shall fall upon you, and inflict the wounds of death in your bodies, that ye may become extinct; and then we shall see who shall have power over this people; yes, we shall see who shall be brought into bondage."

When he heard this, Zerahemnah came forward, and gave his sword and bow and arrows to Moroni. He told Moroni he and his men would deliver up their arms and go home, but they would not promise to stop their wars, because they knew they would break their promise. He told Moroni he did not believe that God had helped them, but thought it was because of the armor and thick clothing of the Nephites that they had been able to win.

Moroni would not end the war in this way. He was determined to make the Lamanites promise not to fight any more. When Zerahemna refused to do so, Moroni gave back the Lamanite general's weapons, and said, "Now as ye are in our hands, we will spill your blood upon the ground, or ye shall submit to the conditions which I have proposed."

The stubborn Zerahemnah took back his sword and then rushed at Moroni, trying to kill him. But as he raised his sword one of the Nephite soldiers struck it out of his hand. As he swung at the Lamanite to save Moroni the Nephite soldier's sword

161

THE ZORAMITE WAR.

grazed the top of Zerahemnah's head, cutting off his scalp. Wounded and bleeding, Zerahemnah ran back to his own soldiers.

The Nephite soldier picked up Zerahemnah's scalp, and put it on the point of his sword. He raised it high above his head, and cried out:

"Even as this scalp has fallen to the earth, which is the scalp of your chief, so shall ye fall to the earth, except ye will deliver up your weapons of war and depart with a covenant of peace."

Many of the Lamanite soldiers, hearing this, came forward and dropped their weapons at Moroni's feet. This made Zerahemnah very angry, and he commanded the rest of his men to attack. So many of the Lamanites were killed when the fight resumed, that Zerahemnah feared his whole army would be lost. He called to Moroni, and promised that if the rest of his soldiers were spared from death, they would all lay down their swords and never fight again.

Moroni stopped his men. All of the Lamanites came forward, putting down their arms, and as each one came he entered a covenant with Moroni never to fight the Nephites again. Then they went away into the wilderness.

162

CHAPTER FIFTY-FIVE

Alma Taken From the Earth

Alma 45.

THE MISSION of Alma, the great prophet, and governor of the Nephites, was nearing its close.

One day he called his son Helaman to his side and said, "Believest thou the words which I spoke unto thee concerning those records which have been kept?" Alma had already made his son the keeper of the records.

Helaman answered, "Yea, I believe."

Then Alma said, "Believest thou in Jesus Christ who shall come?"

And Helaman replied, "Yea, I believe all the words which thou hast spoken."

Then Alma asked, "Will ye keep my commandments?"

"Yea," said Helaman, " I will keep thy commandments with all my heart."

Alma was pleased to hear this. He said to his faithful son, "Blessed art thou, and the Lord shall prosper thee in this land. But behold, I have somewhat to prophesy unto thee; but what I prophesy unto thee shall not be made known, even until the prophecy is fulfilled; therefore write the words which I shall say."

Then he declared that Christ would come as the Savior and that four hundred years afterward the Nephites would become so wicked that they would be destroyed as a nation. Those who would not perish would join the Lamanites. In this way the Nephite nation would cease to exist, he said.

After making this prophesy, Alma called all his sons together and blessed them. He blessed the Church, and all those in it who would remain faithful. He blessed the land also for the righteous, but cursed it for the wicked.

Having said goodbye to his family, Alma left his home. He walked out of Zarahemla toward the city of Melek, but did not reach there. He disappeared from the face of the earth, and was never heard of again. The Nephites did not know what became of him, whether he died, or was taken into heaven.

"But this we know," the *Book of Mormon* record says, "that he was a righteous man; and the saying went abroad in the Church that he was taken up by the Spirit, or buried by the hand of the Lord, even as Moses. But behold, the scriptures saith the Lord took Moses unto himself; and we suppose that he has also received Alma in the spirit unto himself; therefore, for this cause we know nothing concerning his death and burial."

CHAPTER FIFTY-SIX

The Banner of Liberty

Alma 46.

*I*T WAS HARD for the Nephites to learn how to govern themselves. They had been taught that it was best to do their business by the voice of the people, which meant that they should rule themselves. Yet there were some who still thought it was best to have a king.

The members of the Church understood the meaning of liberty, because the prophets had taught them about it. They knew also that to have freedom meant that they could worship the Lord as they wished without a king or his servants preventing them. They loved the Lord and desired to serve him. They did not want some wicked ruler to stop their religious worship. Neither did they want a return of the persecution which had been heaped upon them by wicked people who laughed at their religion. Self-government was a protection to them. They could help make their own laws to protect their rights, both to worship as they pleased, and to do all other things that free people can do.

The wicked who did not belong to the Church did not believe these teachings, and wanted a king. They planned to choose one of their number to rule over them.

One of these men was named Amalickiah. He desired to be the king. He went among the people and tried to stir them up to rebellion. Some of his supporters were the lesser judges of the land, who wanted more power for themselves. Amalickiah promised them that if they would help him overthrow the government, he would give them important positions after he became king.

This caused a division among the people. When Moroni, the commander of the army, heard about it, he was very angry with

Amalickiah. He took off his coat, and tore a large piece out of it, from which he made a flag. On it he wrote these words:

"In memory of our God, our religion, and freedom, and our peace, our wives, and our children."

Putting it on a pole, he called it the title of liberty.

He knew that the people must be taught to protect their liberty, and prevent Amalickiah and his followers from overthrowing the government.

Moroni dressed himself in his battle armor. Then he bowed down in humble prayer to the Lord, asking that liberty might be preserved in the land, so that the righteous could worship without persecution from the people or interference from a wicked king.

He spoke of all the land roundabout as a chosen land, a land of liberty. And he said, "Surely God shall not suffer that we, who are despised because we take upon us the name of Christ, shall be trodden down and destroyed, until we bring it upon us by our own transgressions."

Moroni then went out among the people, waving his banner of liberty so that all who saw it could read what he had written upon it. With a loud voice he said, "Whosoever will maintain this title upon the land, let them come forth in the strength of the Lord, and enter into a covenant that they will maintain their rights, and their religion, that the Lord God may bless them."

The people who loved the Lord put on their armor and rallied to his call. They made the covenant he asked of them, and tore their garments as a sign that they would keep it.

Moroni went into every section of the country where Amalickiah had been, and gathered to his flag all those who were willing to protect their liberty. He soon had more people following him that Amalickiah had. Many of those who had believed Amalickiah's teaching now began to doubt the justice of his cause and deserted him, going over to Moroni's ranks.

When the wicked Amalickiah saw this, he took as many as would follow him, and fled into the wilderness. Moroni did not want them to escape. He feared that they might go over and join the Lamanites, and urge them to start another war against the Nephites. So he went in pursuit and captured most of them. But Amalickiah and a few others escaped. Moroni took his captives back to Zarahemla, where he told them of his covenant of liberty. He wished them to become loyal citizens once more, and to take this oath. Most of them did, but a few refused, still preferring to follow Amalickiah. These were put to death.

The valiant Moroni now went to all parts of the land, establishing freedom wherever he went.

CHAPTER FIFTY-SEVEN

The Treacherous Amalickiah

Alma 47.

*A*MALICKIAH went to the headquarters of the Lamanites, and visited the king. He stirred him up against the Nephites, and urged him to start another war. He talked so convincingly that the king issued a proclamation to his people, commanding them to prepare to fight.

The Lamanites did not want to go to war so soon again. They remembered their last war and their great defeat at the hands of the Nephites, and they feared for their lives if they attacked them again. But they were also afraid of their king, not knowing what he would do if they disobeyed him.

The frightened Lamanites thought the best thing they could do was to run away so that they might escape the king's wrath, and also avoid fighting the Nephites. They went over to Onidah, which was known as the "place of arms."

When the king heard this he was very angry. He gave Amalickiah command over his loyal soldiers and ordered them to make the others obey or slay them all.

Amalickiah was a crafty man, and he was happy with this appointment. In his heart he wished to dethrone the Lamanite king, and then start a war with the Nephites. Getting command of the army helped him in this evil design.

He led the king's soldiers to Onidah where the rest of the Lamanites were. Arriving there he found the people armed and standing on the top of a hill, ready to fight for their lives. Amalickiah would not allow his men to attack. He ordered them to camp for the night.

After dark, he sent a messenger to the commander of the other Lamanites, asking him to come and meet with Amalickiah.

This commander was named Lehonti. He did not trust Amalickiah, and would not come down to the other camp. Three times Amalickiah sent for him, but he still would not come down. Then Amalickiah left his own camp and climbed a little way up the hill to where Lehonti was, and sent a messenger asking Lehonti to come the rest of the way and bring his guards with him if he desired. This time Lehonti came.

Amalickiah had thought of a wicked plan to get control of both armies. He told Lehonti he believed they could be united into one, and that he was willing to help Lehonti bring them together. Lehonti could be the commanding general, but Amalickiah asked to be second in command.

Lehonti could not see anything wrong with this plan, and agreed to it. Amalickiah told Lehonti to bring his men down in the darkness of the night, and surround the king's army which Amalickiah had led. This he did. The next morning the king's soldiers discovered that they had been trapped. Afraid of being killed, the soldiers now asked Amalickiah for permission to join with the other Lamanite army, to avoid a fight. Amalickiah consented, for this would also help him in his plan.

When the two armies were one, Lehonti was made commander of both, and Amalickiah became second in command.

It was the custom among the Lamanites that whenever the commander-in-chief died, the second in command would take his place. Amalickiah knew this. He bribed one of his servants to feed Lehonti poison in small doses, so that he became sick and soon died. The army then proclaimed Amalickiah their leader.

Amalickiah led the armies back to meet the Lamanite king. He was still planning to kill him, and become ruler himself.

As the king came out to greet them, Amalickiah sent some of his soldiers ahead. These men bowed low before the king, who then reached out his hand as a sign of peace, and bade them arise. As they arose they stabbed him.

The king's servants, seeing their master die, ran for their lives, thinking they might be killed too. Amalickiah blamed them for killing the king and sent some of his men to chase them and take their lives. But they escaped, and went to the land of Zarahemla where they joined the Nephites.

Amalickiah and his army camped outside the city that night, but the next day they entered and took possession of it.

The wicked Amalickiah sent a messenger to the queen, telling her of the death of her husband. She asked him to bring witnesses to tell her of the crime. Amalickiah took his men who had actually killed the king, and went into the presence of the queen where they told her that the king was killed by his own servants, who had run away.

As time went on, Amalickiah began to make love to the queen and one day asked her to marry him. She consented, and through this marriage he became king of the Lamanites.

CHAPTER FIFTY-EIGHT

The War Begins

Alma 48, 49 and 50.

AMALICKIAH, now king of the Lamanites, was determined to destroy the Nephites. He told his people many lies about the Nephites, making them so angry that they changed their minds about not starting another war. They decided to fight.

Remembering that in their last war the Nephites had protected themselves with breastplates, helmets, and armor on their arms, and that they had worn clothing heavy enough to protect their bodies from wounds, the Lamanites now did the same thing. With this protection, and with armies which they knew were larger than any the Nephites had, they felt they would win.

Amalickiah appointed as his chief captains men from among the Zoramites, who hated the Nephites even worse than did the Lamanites. He sent them to lead the armies against the Nephites, but he himself did not go with them.

When the Lamanites planned their attack, they thought they would strike first at the city of Ammonihah, which they had destroyed before, and which had been rebuilt by the Nephites. They felt that it would be easy to capture that city.

As they approached it, to their great surprise it had been turned into a fort. Moroni had built high walls around it behind which his men could shoot their arrows and sling their stones at the enemy without being hit themselves.

When they saw these fortifications, the Lamanites decided not to attack. They believed that the nearby land of Noah would be easier to conquer. It had been one of the weak cities of the Nephites, with few soldiers to protect it. But when they got over there, they found it fortified even more strongly than Ammonihah.

Their leaders were ashamed to pass by this city also, and therefore ordered their men to attack. There was only one place where no wall had been built and that was at the entrance to the gates. The Lamanites tried to force their way through there, but were beaten back with heavy losses. Then they tried to dig down the dirt walls about the city, but the Nephites shot them with arrows as they worked, and rolled big stones down upon them from the tops of the earthen walls.

Large numbers of the Lamanites were killed including many of their captains. When the Lamanites saw their leaders die, they stopped fighting and returned to their homes.

Although many of their enemies were killed in this battle, none of the Nephites lost their lives. Some were wounded, but none died. The Nephites thanked the Lord for protecting them.

Moroni was wise in defending his people against the Lamanites. He fortified all of the Nephite cities, and stationed soldiers in each of them. He placed heaps of earth around the cities, and on top of them he built wooden walls as high as a man. These walls had pickets on them for further protection. He also built towers on the earthen walls, from which his men could shoot arrows at their enemies.

Amalickiah was not afraid of the Nephites. He was more determined than ever to come against them. He reorganized his armies and led them against the Nephites himself.

Being more cunning than the Lamanites, Amalickiah was able to conquer some of the Nephite cities. Then he marched toward the land called Bountiful. The Nephites heard of this, and sent an army to stop them. This Nephite army was commanded by one of Moroni's greatest fighters, a man named Teancum.

Teancum's men met the Lamanites in a battle which lasted all day. At night, each army made camp and lay down to rest, expecting to renew the fighting the next morning.

172

But during the night, Teancom crept quietly into the Lamanite camp, where all the tired soldiers were sleeping soundly. He entered the king's tent, and killed him in his sleep. His attack was so quiet that the sleeping guards did not wake up. Then he went back softly to his own camp.

Next morning the Lamanites found Amalickiah dead in his tent. They also saw that Teancum's men were ready to fight so they withdrew to one of the fortified cities they had taken from the Nephites.

Ammoron, brother of Amalickiah, was appointed to be the new king of the Lamanites, and he continued the war.

CHAPTER FIFTY-NINE

An Army Is Trapped

Alma 52-55.

THE CITY of Mulek was captured by the Lamanite army. It was one of the towns which Moroni had fortified, and when the Lamanites took possession of it, they strengthened it even more.

Moroni desired to recapture this city. He sent word to his friend and fellow-warrior, Teancum, to lead an army against Mulek and recapture it.

Teancum was a humble servant of the Lord, and a great Nephite soldier. Like Moroni, his commander, he did all he could to influence the people to love God and keep his commandments. But against the Lamanites, he was a fierce fighter, and defeated them often in battle. It was he who had killed the wicked Lamanite king, Amalickiah.

When Teancum's army reached the city of Mulek, they found it so strongly fortified, and so well defended by a large Lamanite army, that they knew they could never capture it by a direct attack. They would be exposed to the arrows and stones of the enemy, while the Lamanites could hide behind their fortifications.

Teancum led his army back to the land of Bountiful to await the coming of Moroni with more soldiers. When Moroni arrived, he and Teancum called the officers of both armies into a council of war. They decided that in some way the Lamanite army must be brought out of the fortified city, so that the Nephites would be able to fight them in the open.

At first they decided to send a group of soldiers as messengers to the city and ask the Lamanite general to bring his men outside the walls and fight in the open. Of course he refused.

The Nephites then decided to lure the Lamanites out and lead them into a trap. Moroni told Teancum to take a small part of his army, and march past the city of Mulek in full view of the Lamanite army. Moroni at the same time planned to hide his own army near the city during the night to be ready to attack if the Lamanites came out to fight Teancum.

When Teancum led his men past the city toward the sea-shore, which was nearby, the guards inside made haste to tell their commander. They thought Teancum had such a small army there would be no danger in going out to fight them, because their own army was so much larger.

The Lamanite commander looked at the little Nephite army and, like his guards, believed he could go out and destroy it and then return safely to the city.

He ordered his soldiers to leave the protection of the walls, and march against Teancum. As they came, Teancum's men ran toward the sea. The Lamanites followed them until they were far from the city. Then Moroni sent part of his army into the city, capturing it and killing all the Lamanites who were left to guard it. The rest of Moroni's army then hurried after the Lamanites who were chasing Teancum.

As Teancum's army neared the land of Bountiful, they were met by Lehi, another Nephite general, with his army. They joined forces and faced the Lamanites, who turned and ran back toward their city, not knowing it had been captured. Neither did they know that Moroni's army was approaching them from the opposite direction.

Lehi and Teancum did not try to catch up with the fleeing Lamanites at first. They stayed behind until the enemy met Moroni's army, and then attacked. The Lamanites found themselves caught between the two Nephite armies. In the battle Moroni was wounded and the Lamanite commander killed. Lehi and Teancum pressed the Lamanites so hard from the rear that many of the

175

enemy threw down their weapons and stopped fighting. The rest did not know which way to go.

Moroni then told the Lamanites that he would stop the battle if they would lay down their arms. Some of them did, but others would not. Those who refused were captured, and forced to drop their swords. The entire Lamanite army was then taken as prisoners. They were marched back to the land Bountiful, where Moroni made them dig trenches about that city and erect high dirt walls outside the trenches. On the side of the trenches nearest the city, they built high wooden walls. So the Nephites made Bountiful the strongest fort in all the land.

Many prisoners were taken on both sides. The Lamanites had taken not men alone, but women and children from among the Nephites, but the Nephites had captured only the fighting men.

One day the Lamanite king asked Moroni to exchange prisoners. Moroni was glad for this, and determined to get back as many Nephites as possible, also the women and children who had been taken.

He wrote a letter to the Lamanite king, telling him that he would exchange prisoners, but on one condition: That for each Lamanite prisoner returned, he demanded a Nephite soldier and also the soldier's wife and children.

This pleased the Lamanite king, because he found it hard to feed so many prisoners. But when he replied to Moroni, he lied about the Nephites which so angered Moroni that he refused to exchange prisoners with the Lamanites.

Moroni tried to find a way to rescue the Nephite prisoners without giving back any of the Lamanites he had captured. After searching through his army for a trusted man of Lamanite blood, he found one of the servants of the Lamanite king who had been killed by Amalickiah. He and the other servants had gone to the Nephites for protection when their king was killed. This servant's name was Laman. Moroni called him and a few others together,

176

and told them of his plan to save the prisoners. He gave them pitchers of wine and told them to go at night among the Lamanites who were guarding the city of Gid where the prisoners were kept, and make them drunk.

Taking the wine, Laman and his helpers went to the city. When they met the guards, Laman told them he was a Lamanite and that he brought them wine to drink. The guards were glad for the wine and wanted to drink it at once. Laman urged them to wait until they went into battle, but this made the Lamanites crave the wine even more. Laman then gave it to them, and they drank so much that they fell into a drunken sleep.

Laman hurried back to Moroni and told him what had happened. Moroni then sent soldiers to Gid. They armed all the Nephite prisoners with swords and other weapons and told them to remain quiet within the city until morning. Then Moroni brought an army to surround the city on the outside.

In the morning, when the Lamanites woke, they found their city surrounded on the outside by a Nephite army, and then much to their surprise they saw that all of the prisoners were armed and ready to fight. They laid down their weapons and surrendered to Moroni. The Nephite prisoners joined Moroni's army and greatly increased its strength.

CHAPTER SIXTY

The Sons of Helaman

Alma 53, 56-57.

*T*HE PEOPLE of Ammon had been Lamanites. Ammon and his brethren had preached the gospel to them, and they became faithful members of the Church. As part of their conversion to Christ, they promised that they would never again go to war. They buried their weapons in the ground, left their homes, and came to Zarahemla where they joined the Nephites.

In the bitter fighting between the Nephites and the Lamanites, many faithful men were killed or taken prisoner, and this greatly weakened the Nephite armies.

The people of Ammon knew this. They also knew that many of the Nephites had been killed while protecting them.

When the people of Ammon saw the sufferings of the Nephites, who had been so kind to them, they decided to break their promise and help the Nephites in the war.

The Prophet Helaman, son of Alma, felt this would not be wise. He told them that they must keep the covenants they had made, and never fight again. They took his advice, and none of the men who had made this promise ever did go to war again. But they still desired to help in some way.

During the years when they had lived among the Nephites, many sons were born to them. These sons had not taken the oath against war. They were free to fight in defense of their homes and give aid to the hard-pressed Nephite armies.

The young men gathered in a meeting. Although they were born of Lamanite parents, they now took upon themselves the name of Nephites, because they had been converted to Christ by the Nephites, and had become one with them.

178

They also made a covenant among themselves to fight for the liberty of the Nephites and to protect their own homes. They made a solemn promise that they would never give up their liberty, but would fight to protect the Nephites and themselves from bondage among the Lamanites.

There were two thousand of these young men. After deciding to fight, they armed themselves with weapons of war, and prepared to join the Nephite army. But they asked that Helaman the prophet be their leader.

Helaman gladly accepted and called them his sons. They were courageous young men, not afraid to fight or to die. But most important of all, they believed sincerely in the Lord, and could be trusted to perform fully any task that was given to them.

Before they left for the war, their mothers taught them great faith in God, promising that if they did not doubt, God would protect them.

Helaman led his army of boys away to war. He planned to march to the city of Judea to join forces with an army commanded by Antipus, which was weak and discouraged. They became a great strength to Antipus and his men. But when the Lamanites saw that Antipus was reinforced by this army of two thousand, they would not attack the city. Many days passed, and still there was no attack by the Lamanites. Then the fathers of the two thousand young men brought provisions to their sons. This also cheered the Nephites, but worried the Lamanites, who began to send out soldiers to prevent more supplies from reaching the Nephites.

Seeing the anxiety of the Lamanites, Antipus and Helaman decided to draw them out of their city into open country for the battle.

Antipus ordered Helaman to take his two thousand young men and march to a nearby city, making it appear as if they were carrying supplies. It was hoped that the Lamanite army would come out of its fortified city and follow them. The army of Antipus would then come up behind and try to trap the Lamanite army in the same way Moroni had trapped another Lamanite force at the city of Mulek.

Helaman and his men started out, marching past the Lamanite city. The Lamanites came out after them, and as they came, the sons of Helaman ran before them, trying to get them away from their city. All that day the Lamanites followed them, but could not catch them. The chase continued for two days more. Still the Lamanites could not overtake these young men.

When Antipus saw the Lamanites follow Helaman on the first day, he led his soldiers out to follow behind the Lamanites, but the Lamanites did not know they were being pursued.

On the third day, Helaman noticed that the Lamanites were no longer following. He supposed that Antipus and his men had caught up with them, and that they were at that moment fighting.

Calling his two thousand young men about him, he asked them if they would return and fight the Lamanites, giving relief to Antipus and his men.

These boys thought more of their liberty than they did of their lives. When asked to fight they told Helaman about the promise made to them by their mothers. If they did not doubt the Lord, he would protect them. That was their faith.

Helaman then led them back. Soon they saw fighting going on between the Lamanites and the army of Antipus. The Nephites were tired from their fast chase after the Lamanites, and although they fought well, the Lamanites were defeating them in battle. Antipus was killed, as were other Nephite leaders. With no commander to direct them, the soldiers were confused and were beginning to give way to the Lamanites as the sons of Helaman came up. The young men attacked the Lamanites with fury. Never had Helaman seen such fighting. As soon as they attacked, the whole

The young men attacked the Lamanites with fury

Lamanite army turned upon them, leaving the tired army of Antipus for the moment.

When the army of Antipus saw that help had arrived, they took courage, and once more entered the fight. The Lamanites were now caught between the two Nephite armies, and soon surrendered.

At the close of the battle, Helaman counted his young men to see if any had been killed. Not one had died. Afterward, in telling Moroni about the conflict, Helaman wrote:

"And now it came to pass that when they (the Lamanites) had surrendered themselves up unto us, behold I numbered those young men who had fought with me, fearing lest there were many of them slain. But behold, to my great joy, there was not one soul of them fallen to the earth; yea, and they had fought with such miraculous strength; and with such mighty power did they fall upon the Lamanites that they did frighten them; and for this cause did the Lamanites deliver themselves up as prisoners of war."

CHAPTER SIXTY-ONE

Rebellion at Home

Alma 60-62.

*W*HEN fighting the Lamanites, the Nephite armies were far from their city of Zarahemla. It was from there that their food and other supplies were to be brought to them.

Moroni, the general, began to find his army short of supplies. He sent back asking for more food and other help. None came. Moroni became angry. He wrote to Pahoran, the chief judge, demanding more supplies and saying he could not continue the fight without them. Moroni said unless the supplies came at once, he would return with his army and punish Pahoran and the others at home for failing to send what they needed.

Pahoran replied to Moroni, with bad news. While the main strength of the Nephite forces was engaged in fighting the Lamanites, a group of rebels at home in Zarahemla had started trouble there. They wanted to overthrow the government.

Pahoran could not overcome these trouble-makers who persuaded many in the city to join them. They appointed one of their leaders as king, and drove Pahoran and his men out of the city, taking control of it themselves. This king was named Pachus. When he got possession of the city he sent a messenger to the king of the Lamanites, and offered to form an alliance with him to help the Lamanites gain control over the rest of the country.

Pahoran, in his letter, begged Moroni to bring a part of the Nephite army back to Zarahemla to defeat these rebels, who were preventing him from sending the supplies which Moroni needed. He asked Moroni to leave Teancum and Lehi in charge of the war against the Lamanites, while he came back to put down the rebellion.

When Moroni received the letter from Pahoran, he was glad

in spite of the bad news it contained. He had feared that Pahoran himself had turned traitor, but now he knew the chief judge was loyal and true.

He turned command of the Nephite armies over to Lehi and Teancum, and took a small force with him back toward Zarahemla. On the way he called at other Nephite cities, and raising again his standard of liberty, recruited many more soldiers to help him in the cause of freedom.

Pahoran had escaped to the city of Gideon when Pachus drove him out of Zarahemla. Moroni led his new army to this city, where he joined forces with Pahoran. Then they marched against Zarahemla, determined to recapture it and punish Pachus and his rebels.

Pachus and his soldiers went out to meet them, and a battle began, in which Pachus and many of his followers were killed. Those who were left alive were taken prisoners by Moroni, who marched into the city and restored the power of government to Pahoran.

A trial was held for the followers of Pachus who had been captured, and they were all sentenced to death as traitors.

Moroni immediately formed a supply train to take food and other necessities to the armies which were away fighting the Lamanites. He enlisted more men for the army and sent six thousand to Helaman to strengthen him and his two thousand "sons." He also sent another six thousand men to Lehi and Teancum, together with a large supply of food.

Many of the Lamanites who surrendered during the war asked permission of Moroni to go into the land of Jershon and there join the people of Ammon who had made a covenant never to fight again. They promised to make the same covenant as had the people of Ammon, and said they would be one with them.

Moroni gave this permission. But he made them work for the Nephites, raising crops and making supplies to be sent to the Nephite soldiers.

CHAPTER SIXTY-TWO

Teancum Is Killed

Alma 62.

*T*EANCUM was one of the greatest soldiers among the Nephites. He, Moroni and Lehi were the three leading generals of the Nephite armies.

Teancum wanted to end the costly war in which his people were engaged with the Lamanites. He blamed Amalickiah and his brother Ammoron for the whole trouble.

These two men had been Nephites, but had gone over to the Lamanites. They joined the enemy because Amalickiah hoped to be made king over the Nephites and started a rebellion among them. Later he killed the Lamanite king, and became king in his place. Then he started the war with the Nephites.

Teancum had met Amalickiah in battle, and at night crept into the Lamanite camp and killed him while he slept. But that had not ended the war because Amalickiah's brother Ammoron became king in his place, and carried on even more bitterly than his brother had.

Teancum thought that if Ammoron were killed, the Lamanites might be willing to stop the war. Ammoron was carrying it on as revenge for the death of his brother.

The Lamanites were encamped inside one of the walled cities they had captured. King Ammoron was with them. Teancum decided to try to kill Ammoron while he slept, as he had killed his brother Amalickiah.

Late at night, when all were asleep, he took a long rope and climbed to the top of the city wall. He fastened one end of his rope to the wall, and lowered himself on the inside. He had no idea where the king's tent was, so he went from place to place, stepping quietly until at last he found it. Entering, he saw the king and his guards sound asleep. He threw a javelin at the sleeping king, hoping to strike him in the heart and kill him instantly. But his aim was poor. He struck the king in the chest, but did not hit his heart. The king awoke and roused his guards before he died. The guards ran after Teancum, and before the brave Nephite could get to his rope on the wall, the Lamanites overtook him and killed him.

When Moroni and Lehi heard what had happened they grieved greatly. They loved Teancum; he had been valiant in fighting for his country, and was a true friend of liberty. He had served his people well.

The Nephites determined to follow up the advantage Teancum had given them. Without a king to lead them, the enemy would be easier to defeat.

Moroni and Lehi ordered their men to attack the Lamanites early the next morning, and defeated them so completely that they did not come against the Nephites again for several years. The Nephite armies were able to return home, and peace was established in the land. Helaman went back to his work of preaching the gospel from city to city.

Having suffered so much in this war, the Nephites were very humble. They served the Lord, and he blessed them and they again began to prosper.

CHAPTER SIXTY-THREE

The Land Northward

Alma 63, Helaman 3.

*A*MERICA as it was known to the Nephites was divided into two parts, a land to the north and a land to the south. The two parts were connected by a "narrow neck of land."

The people of Lehi had first settled in the "land southward." The people of Jared, who were destroyed in their great civil war, had lived in the "land northward." It was there that the scouts of King Limhi found their records.

When the long war ended, and the Nephites again began to enjoy peace, some of them decided to go into the "land northward" to make their homes. While at first only a few went, later many people followed them. In one company there were fifty-four hundred men, with their wives and children. They all left Zarahemla, and went to the north land.

One of the men most interested in settling this new country was named Hagoth. He was a very curious man, and a ship-builder. He believed that the people could go northward in ships more easily than they could go by land, and he decided to build ships so that any of the Nephites who wished could sail along the seacoast, past the narrow neck of land, and enter some harbor in the land northward to make their homes.

On the seashore near the land Bountiful, not far from the narrow neck of land, he built a large ship.

When it was ready, many of the Nephites wanted to sail north in it. They brought their wives and children, with their provisions, and boarded Hagoth's ship to begin their voyage.

The next year the ship returned. Many more people wanted to sail northward and they brought their provisions and their families and set sail, hoping to reach the "land northward" as had

187

HAGOTH BUILDS A LARGE SHIP.

those who went on the first voyage. But the ship never reached there. No one heard of them after they left the land Bountiful in Hagoth's ship. The Nephites supposed that the ship must have sunk with all of its passengers.

Another ship was loaded with passengers for the northward journey, and set out to sea. But neither was it heard of again. This did not discourage the people, and still more went northward and made their homes.

There are ocean currents leading into the Pacific Ocean from the American west coast, near where it is believed the land Bountiful was. These currents go far out and reach to Hawaii and other small islands in the south seas.

The Hawaiians, the New Zealanders, the Samoans, and other islanders, have traditions among them which tell that their forefathers came from a land far to the east, and that they were white people. It is believed that some of the Nephites or Lamanites may have drifted in their boats away from the American coast, and were carried by these ocean currents to the islands of the south seas.

Modern sailors have drifted in boats or rafts from the American coasts directly to these same South Sea Islands.

In the period of peace during which these migrations northward took place, both Moroni, the general, and Helaman, the prophet, died. The son of Helaman, whose name was also Helaman, took the sacred records, and carried on the work of his father. He too was a righteous man, and became a great prophet among the Nephites.

In the days of the younger Helaman, many more people went northward, beyond the narrow neck of land, there to build cities and farms.

There were very few trees in the land northward, so the people had to find materials other than wood from which to build their houses. Some they built of stone, but many of them of cement. These ancient peoples learned the art of working in cement, and made not only houses but large buildings for other purposes, some of which may be seen to this day in central America and Mexico. They built temples on the top of high pyramids.

Many people began to go northward. Even the followers of Ammon, the people who once had been Lamanites and then were converted by Ammon and his brethren, felt the urge to move, and many of them left their homes in the land of Jershon and moved north.

CHAPTER SIXTY-FOUR

Gadianton the Robber

Helaman 1 and 2.

*I*N THE DAYS of the second Helaman, there lived two very wicked Nephites, named Gadianton and Kishkumen. They were murderers at heart and wished to rob people, and if necessary take their lives in order to get their money or their positions.

Satan directed these two men. He taught them the evil ways he showed to Cain, the son of Adam and Eve. He had led Cain to murder his brother in order to get his sheep. He also had taught other men to commit crimes to get worldly goods, and told them how to keep their wicked secrets, and protect each other in their sins.

Gadianton and Kishkumen planned to overthrow the government of the land of Zarahemla. When Pahoran, the close friend of Moroni the general, became sick and died, his son, also named Pahoran, was elected by the people to succeed his father as the chief judge and governor.

Kishkumen thought this change would be a good time to carry out his evil scheme. He disguised himself and crept into the governor's house and killed him while he sat in judgment. The servants of the governor chased the murderer, but could not run as fast as Kishkumen, so he escaped. He got back to his friends and told them what he had done, and they took an oath never to tell anyone that Kishkumen had killed the governor. Then the members of the evil group went among the people so that no one would suspect them.

Another son of Pahoran now was elected to be governor and judge. His name was Pacumeni. A short time after he was chosen, he was killed by Lamanites who attacked the city. After these

Lamanites were driven out another election was held and Helaman, the son of Helaman, friend of Moroni, was chosen governor.

Gadianton and Kishkumen did not like Helaman, who was a righteous man and an officer of the Church, and planned to kill him also. They gathered their band of wicked men together and took an oath to protect each other in the crimes which they expected to commit.

Gadianton was a cunning man, and he became the leader of this robber band. He told the bandits that if they would make him governor, he would place them in positions of high authority in the government.

Kishkumen was flattered when he heard how much authority he would have if Gadianton were made the governor. When the band plotted to kill Helaman, Kishkumen agreed to go to the house of the governor and take his life.

But one of Helaman's servants had been sent out as a spy to learn what Gadianton and his men were plotting. He had disguised himself, so that the robbers did not know he was a servant of Helaman.

The robbers had a sign or signal which they gave whenever they saw each other outside of their meetings. In this way they kept close together, and showed that they were members of the band, and were keeping secret their evil oaths.

The servant of Helaman discovered what this sign was. He also learned that Kishkumen was going to the hall of government to try to kill Helaman. Later, no longer in disguise, but dressed as the governor's servant, he met Kishkumen on his way to find Helaman, and gave him the secret sign.

Happy to find that one of the servants of the governor was a member of the secret band of Gadianton robbers, Kishkumen made friends with him, and told of his plan to kill Helaman. He asked the servant to lead him to the hall of judgment, so that he could carry out his plan.

The servant, who was loyal and true to Helaman, said to Kishkumen, "Let us go forth unto the judgment seat."

This pleased the robber, who now thought that his evil work would be made easy. But as they were walking along together, the servant quickly took out his dagger and stabbed Kishkumen in the heart. The robber fell dead without a sound.

The servant then ran to Helaman and told him what had happened, and Helaman sent out his guards to try to find the other robbers and arrest them. But when Kishkumen did not return at once, Gadianton knew something had gone wrong, and he and the others of his band escaped into the wilderness. By the time Helaman's guards arrived at the robbers' meeting place, they had all left.

While hiding in the wilderness from Helaman's men, Gadianton and his robber band planned to bring more of the Nephites into their organization, hoping to become strong enough to take over the government for themselves.

CHAPTER SIXTY-FIVE

Zarahemla Captured

Helaman 4.

ABOUT thirty-five years before the birth of the Savior, the Nephites were living in peace. The Lord blessed them, and as a result they became very prosperous. But as had happened before, they now began to love their money and fine clothing more than they loved the Lord.

Some of them quarrelled among themselves, and grew very bitter in their feelings. Others fought the Church and its members and persecuted them.

There were some who became so evil that they wanted to destroy all of the righteous Nephites.

Traitors at heart, these wicked Nephites went over among the Lamanites and tried to get them to start a war. But the Lamanites did not want to fight. They were tired of war, and wanted to live in peace. But the traitors from the Nephites told them many lies, and they began to grow very angry toward the Nephites, and decided to fight them.

The Lamanites prepared all year for the coming battles, while the Nephites had no thought of war, and made no such preparation. At the end of the year, the Lamanites struck against the unsuspecting Nephites, and killed many of them. In previous wars they had attacked first on the outskirts of the land of Zarahemla. This time, they invaded the very center of the Nephite country, and drove the Nephites from their homes. They came against the city of Zarahemla, the capital of the nation, and captured it. Some of the people who lived there escaped to Bountiful, which was near the narrow neck of land leading into the northern part of the country. They then moved into this region to the north.

At this time the commander of the Nephite armies was Mor-

193

onihah. As he saw city after city fall into the hands of the Lamanites, and knew that the enemy was more numerous than themselves, he realized that the whole land southward would have to
be abandoned. He quickly built a line of forts across the southern
entrance to the narrow neck of land and as soon it was ready,
the Nephites in the land southward hurried behind it for protection. The distance across this narrow neck of land was spoken
of as being a day's journey for a Nephite.

For two years the Lamanites held the Nephites behind this
line of forts. But in the third year of the war, Moronihah formed
a strong army which he led into the land southward. He began
to recapture many of the old Nephite cities. One after another fell
into his hands. At last about one-half of the cities taken by the
Lamanites were recaptured by Moronihah. But it was a costly war
in which many lives were lost.

Moronihah was a righteous man. He knew that the sufferings
which had come from this new war were the result of the evil
ways of the Nephites who had turned away from the Lord when
they became prosperous.

Knowing that he could not continue to hold back the Lamanites without the help of the Lord, Moronihah began to preach to
the Nephites, hoping that they would repent. But they would not
listen to him. Even among the members of the Church there were
those who turned away from the Lord, and no longer believed
the prophecies of the scriptures.

For two more years Moronihah fought the Lamanites and
preached repentance to his own people. But he was not successful in either effort. The Lamanites attacked his men in ever growing numbers, and he had to retreat farther and farther. At last
he gave up all hope of recapturing the rest of their cities south of
the narrow neck of land. The Lamanites were too numerous, and
his own people were too wicked to win their battles. He did not
know what the end would be.

CHAPTER SIXTY-SIX

A Mission for Peace

Helaman 5.

*H*ELAMAN, the son of Helaman, had two sons, named Nephi and Lehi. They were good young men who loved the Lord and served him. When their father died, Nephi was given the sacred records, and was chosen judge and governor of the Nephites.

Nephi, like Moronihah, the general, knew that without the blessings of the Lord, the Nephites would be destroyed by the Lamanites or become slaves to them.

Nephi, as judge and governor, saw the wickedness of his people and grew weary of it. He and his brother Lehi remembered the teachings of their father, who was a great prophet to the people.

The two brothers now decided to go on a mission in the hope of bringing their people to repentance. Nephi gave up the position of judge and governor, and he and Lehi began a missionary journey in which they planned to preach to all of the Nephites. They went first to Bountiful, and from there to the city of Gid, and then to the city of Mulek.

After this they went among the Lamanites. The Lord blessed them with his spirit so that they spoke with great power to the Lamanites, and many believed what they said. In the region about Zarahemla, eight thousand Lamanites were converted and baptized.

After performing this great work in Zarahemla, the two brothers went deep into the Lamanite country. Hardly had they reached there than they were captured by Lamanite soldiers who threw them into the same prison where Ammon and his brethren had been placed when they came among the people of King Lamoni. Nephi and Lehi were kept there for days without food.

195

One day the soldiers came for them, to kill them. As they entered the prison, to their surprise they saw a circle of fire about the two missionaries. It did not burn the prison, neither did it hurt the missionaries, and yet they saw that it was fire. The Lamanites were afraid and did not come closer.

When Nephi and Lehi saw that they were surrounded by this heavenly fire, and that the Lamanites were afraid of it, they were thankful to the Lord for sending it. They spoke to the frightened Lamanites, saying, "Fear not, for behold, it is God that has shown unto you this marvelous thing, in the which is shown unto you that ye cannot lay your hands on us to slay us."

When they said this, the Lord sent an earthquake which shook the prison, but the walls did not fall down.

There were other prisoners there, some of whom were Lamanites and some Nephites who had come to join the Lamanites, but were put in prison.

A cloud of darkness now came into the prison, making the Lamanites even more frightened. Then a voice was heard, saying, "Repent ye, repent ye, and seek no more to destroy my servants whom I have sent unto you to declare good tidings."

It was not a loud voice, but was soft and mild, almost like a whisper, and yet it pierced the souls of all who were there. It also shook the earth again, and the walls of the prison trembled. The voice spoke three times.

Among those in the prison was a Nephite who once belonged to the Church but had apostatized. He looked through the dark cloud toward Nephi and Lehi and saw their faces shining through the darkness like the faces of angels. He saw that their eyes were turned heavenward, as though they were talking to some heavenly being.

This Nephite, whose name was Aminadab, called to the others in the prison and told them to look at Nephi and Lehi as their faces shone so brightly through the dark cloud. They looked and

196

Lehi and Nephi in prison . .

M.E.Swensen

saw what Aminadab had seen. They asked him, "What do all these things mean? And who is it with whom these men do converse?"

"They do converse with the angels of God," he replied.

Then the Lamanites asked, "What shall we do that this cloud of darkness may be removed from overshadowing us?"

Aminadab answered, "You must repent, and cry unto the voice, even until ye shall have faith in Christ, who was taught unto you by Alma, and Amulek, and Zeezrom; and then the cloud of darkness shall be removed from overshadowing you."

All those in the prison then began to pray, and they prayed until the dark cloud went away. When it had gone, the heavenly fire which surrounded Nephi and Lehi now came about them. The fire looked like flames, but it did not hurt them, neither did it set fire to the walls of the prison. Those who were encircled with the fire were filled with the Spirit of God. They were filled with joy also and under the inspiration of the Holy Spirit they spoke many wonderful things.

The heavenly voice came again, and said, "Peace, peace be unto you, because of your faith in my Well Beloved."

As they listened to this voice, they looked up in the direction from which it came, and they saw the heavens open, and angels came down and ministered to them.

About three hundred persons were in the prison and saw all these things. They were now told to go out among the people of the city, and tell them what they had seen and heard. They did so, and most of the Lamanites who lived near were converted by their preaching. All who were converted laid down their weapons of war, and would not fight again.

They were in possession of many of the Nephite cities which they had captured. Now, after their conversion, they moved out and gave these cities back to the Nephites.

So many of the Lamanites were converted that they became a better people than the Nephites. The members of the Church among the Nephites were thankful to the Lord for the conversion of the Lamanites, and welcomed them into the Church.

Many of the converted Lamanites now came among the wicked Nephites and preached to them. They went to the city of Zarahemla, and taught them repentance.

Then, together with Nephi and Lehi, they went to the land northward, and continued preaching there. So many of the Nephites believed, peace came throughout all the land. The Nephites could travel among the Lamanites, and the Lamanites could travel among the Nephites, in perfect safety. Both peoples began to till their farms, mine precious metals, and manufacture many kinds of clothing and jewelry, and once more they prospered.

CHAPTER SIXTY-SEVEN

Gadianton Gains Control

Helaman 6 to 8.

GADIANTON and Kishkumen had organized a band of robbers in the city of Zarahemla. They plotted to overthrow the government, and place Gadianton at its head. Kishkumen tried to kill Helaman, the chief judge, but was killed himself by one of Helaman's servants. Then Gadianton and his followers fled into the wilderness.

While they were in hiding there, they made plans to bring more men into their band. They sent their members secretly among the Nephites, persuading all who were greedy for either money or power, or all who loved sin and darkness, to join them. Many of the Nephites did so.

They also sent out other members to work among the Lamanites, to persuade them to join also. If Nephites and Lamanites joined, Gadianton could control both.

As soon as the leaders of the Lamanites learned what Gadianton was doing, they sent soldiers to capture as many of the robbers as possible and kill them. Now that the Lamanites had accepted the gospel, they loved the Lord, and they knew that the truth was even more powerful than the sword. So they began to preach the gospel to those of their number who had joined the robbers. They converted them, and brought them back into the Church. They continued their work until there were no more Gadianton robbers among the Lamanites.

But a great many of the Nephites joined. The Nephites were now more wicked than the Lamanites. Only the most faithful members of the Church kept the commandments of the Lord; the others were proud and sinful; they loved money; they oppressed the poor and humble, and they cheated and robbed each other.

Because they were so sinful, they were glad to join the Gadianton band which, they thought, would protect them from being punished when they broke the law.

One day, the governor of Zarahemla, whose name was Cezoram, was killed while he sat in the judgment seat. The truth about his murder was not made clear, nor who committed it.

The son of Cezoram was elected by the people to succeed his father, but hardly had he been chosen than he also was killed by an assassin. Nor would anyone tell who had done this.

The killers were members of the Gadianton band, who were still trying to control the government. Because so many of the Nephites had joined Gadianton, they were able to keep secret the names of the men who had committed the murders.

Before long, more than half of the Nephites were members of his band. Then Gadianton seized control of the government. Having the power, he persecuted the members of the Church, and oppressed the poor. The robbers continued to protect each other in their crimes, and committed sins of all kinds.

At this time, Nephi, the son of Helaman, who had gone northward on a missionary journey, returned to the city of Zarahemla. He had been preaching to the people north of the narrow neck of land, but they were so wicked there also that they would not listen to him, and drove him out of their cities.

When he arrived in Zarahemla, and saw the wickedness of the people, and learned that Gadianton and his robber band had obtained control of the government, he was deeply grieved.

He wished that he had lived in earlier days, when the people were faithful to the Lord. But, he said, "I am consigned that these are my days and that my soul shall be filled with sorrow, because of this the wickedness of my brethren."

In Nephi's garden was a tower to which he went at times to pray. This garden was near the main highway which led to the market place in the city of Zarahemla. The tower was near the garden gate, facing the highway.

Nephi mourned greatly because of the sinfulness of the people. In sorrow he climbed the tower in his garden, and poured out his soul to the Lord in prayer.

Some men who were passing by on the highway saw him there, and noticed that he was in deep grief. They hurried into the city, and called others also to come and see. They did so, and wondered why anybody should mourn as Nephi did. A large crowd assembled near the tower, watching him.

When Nephi ended his prayer, and arose to his feet, he saw the people who had gathered, and said, "Why have ye gathered yourselves together? That I may tell you of your iniquities?"

He told them that because of his grief he had climbed the tower to pray to God, and he said he sorrowed because of their wickedness. "And because of my mourning and lamentation," he said, "ye have gathered yourselves together, and do marvel; yea, ye ought to marvel because ye are given away that the devil has got so great hold upon your hearts. Yea, how could you have given away to the enticing of him who is seeking to hurl away your souls down to everlasting misery and endless wo?"

Then he appealed to them to repent of their sins, for he said if they continued on in sin, the Lord would destroy them and "he shall scatter you forth that ye shall become meat for dogs and wild beasts."

He told them that it was because of their greed for money that they had turned away from the Lord. He said that if they did not repent, the Lord would not strengthen them nor protect them when the Lamanites came against them in war; he said their city would be taken from them, and all of their possessions.

CHAPTER SIXTY-EIGHT

Nephi Accused of Murder

Helaman 8 and 9.

*I*NCLUDED in the crowd of wicked people listening to Nephi preach from his tower were members of the Gadianton robbers, lesser judges in the court. Nephi knew this, and spoke with sharpness to them, warning them of the destruction which would come upon them, and telling them of the evils of Gadianton's band.

"Ye are ripening for destruction," he cried out to them. "Yea, behold it is now even at your doors; yea, go ye in unto the judgment seat, and search; and behold your judge is murdered, and he lieth in his blood; and he hath been murdered by his brother, who seeketh to sit in the judgment seat. And behold, they both belong to your secret band, whose author is Gadianton and the evil one who seeketh to destroy the souls of men."

Inspired of the Lord, Nephi had told them something they did not know. Their judge had been killed — and by his brother, who wanted to rule in his place. They could not believe it, and five men went to investigate.

The five ran as fast as they could to the hall of judgment, and as they went they said, "Now we will know of a surety whether this man be a prophet, and God hath commanded him to prophesy such marvelous things unto us. Behold, we do not believe that he hath, yea, we do not believe that he is a prophet; nevertheless, if this thing which he hath said concerning the chief judge be true, then will we believe that the other words which he has spoken are true.

Running swiftly, they came into the judgment hall, and there they found the judge, lying dead.

So surprised were they when they saw it, and so frightened did they become, knowing that all the other things Nephi had said

203

must also be true, that they fainted and fell near the body of the chief judge.

The brother of the chief judge had come into the judgment hall in disguise, so that no one knew him. After killing the judge, he ran into the street to hide. When the servants of the judge discovered the crime, they also ran out, and called the people to come and see what had happened.

While the servants were out calling the people, the five men had come in from listening to Nephi. When the crowd assembled they found the five men lying there, unconscious, and thought they were the ones who had killed the judge. The people near the governor's palace knew nothing of the gathering near Nephi's house.

When they saw the five men lying near the body of the judge, they said, "These men are they who have murdered the judge, and God has smitten them that they could not flee from us."

They tied up all of them, and threw them into prison. Then a proclamation was issued, saying that the judge had been killed and his slayers had been captured.

The next day, a public funeral service was held for the dead judge. Among those who attended were the lesser judges who had been at Nephi's home the day before and heard what the prophet said. They asked others at the funeral what had become of the five men they had sent from Nephi's home to see whether the judge had been killed. The others answered, "Concerning the five whom ye say ye have sent, we know not; but there are five who are the murderers, whom we have cast into prison."

The lesser judges asked that the five men be brought in so they could see them, and when they were brought in, they were the same whom they had sent. The judges asked them to explain what had happened.

They said, "We ran and came to the place of judgment, and when we saw all things, even as Nephi had testified, we were astonished, insomuch that we fell to the earth; and when we were recovered from our astonishment, behold they cast us into prison. Now as for the murder of this man, we know not who has done it, and only this much we know, we ran and came according as ye desired, and behold he was dead, according to the words of Nephi."

The judges then told the people that Nephi had told them the judge was slain, and they accused Nephi of committing the murder because he knew about it before they did.

They said, "We know that this Nephi must have agreed with some one to slay the judge, and then he might declare unto us, that he might convert us unto his faith, that he might raise himself to be a great man, chosen of God, and a prophet. And now behold, we will detect this man, and he shall confess his fault and make known unto us the true murderer of this judge."

The five men were then released, but they rebuked the lesser judges for accusing Nephi falsely. An argument between them and the judges began and they confounded the judges.

But in their anger, the lesser judges had Nephi arrested and brought before the people for trial. They questioned him in many ways, to make him admit that he had killed the judge. They even offered him money, saying that if he had a confederate in the crime, he would be paid for revealing his name.

Nephi was not afraid. He said, "O ye fools, ye blind, ye stiff-necked people, do ye know how long the Lord your God will suffer you that ye shall go on in this your way of sin?"

Then he continued, "Ye say that I have agreed with a man that he should murder Seezoram, our chief judge. But behold, I say unto you, that this is because I have testified unto you concerning this thing; yea, even for a witness unto you, that I did know of the wickedness and abominations which are among you. And because I have done this, ye say that I have agreed with a man

205

that he should do this thing; yea, because I showed you this sign, ye are angry with me, and seek to destroy my life."

"And now behold," said Nephi, "I will show unto you another sign, and see if ye will in this thing seek to destroy me.

"Behold I say unto you: Go to the house of Seantum, who is the brother of Seezoram, and say unto him, Has Nephi, the pretended prophet, who doth prophesy so much evil concerning this people, agreed with thee, in the which ye have murdered Seezoram, who is your brother? And behold he shall say, Nay. And ye shall say unto him, Have ye murdered your brother? And he shall stand with fear, and wist not what to say. And behold he shall deny unto you; and he shall make as if he were astonished. Nevertheless he shall declare unto you that he is innocent.

"But behold, ye shall examine him, and ye shall find blood upon the skirts of his cloak. And when ye have seen this, ye shall say, From whence cometh this blood? Do we not know that this is the blood of your brother? And then he shall tremble, and shall look pale, even as if death had come upon him. And then ye shall say, Because of this fear and this paleness, which has come upon your face, behold, we know that thou art guilty. And then shall greater fear come upon him, and then shall he confess unto you, and deny no more that he has done this murder. And then shall he say unto you, that I, Nephi, know nothing concerning the matter, save it were given unto me by the power of God. And then shall ye know that I am an honest man, and that I am sent unto you from God."

The people hurried to the home of the judge's brother, and all that Nephi said to them came true. The brother did at first deny, then confessed, just as Nephi said he would.

Some of the Nephites believed in God as a result of this event, but many others were so hard in their hearts they would not accept either the teachings of Nephi, or the testimony of the five men who found the judge dead as Nephi had predicted.

CHAPTER SIXTY-NINE

The Lord Speaks to Nephi

Helaman 10.

*A*s Nephi finished speaking to the wicked people in the hall of judgment, they left, many of them to go to the home of the judge's brother. At last he stood alone in the hall.

Pondering upon the wonderful thing the Lord had done for him, he walked slowly home. He knew that the Lord had given him revelations about the death of the judge. Only the Lord could put those words into his mouth. Only the Lord had spared him from the mob, and exposed the true murderer.

As he was thinking about this, a voice spoke to him. It was the voice of the Lord, and it said, "Blessed art thou, Nephi, for those things which thou hast done; for I have beheld how thou hast with unwearyingness declared the word which I have given unto thee, unto this people. And thou hast not feared them, and hast not sought thine own life, but have sought my will, and to keep my commandments.

"And now because thou hast done this with such unwearyingness, behold, I will bless thee forever; and I will make thee mighty in word and in deed, in faith and in works; yea, even that all things shall be done unto thee according to thy word, for thou shalt not ask that which is contrary to my will.

"Behold, thou art Nephi, and I am God. Behold, I declare it unto thee in the presence of mine angels, that ye shall have power over this people, and shall smite the earth with famine, and with pestilence, and destruction, according to the wickedness of this people.

"Behold, I give unto you power, that whatsoever ye shall seal on earth, shall be sealed in heaven; and whatsoever ye shall loose on earth, shall be loosed in heaven; and thus shall ye have power among this people.

"And if ye shall say unto this temple, it shall be rent in twain, it shall be done. And if ye shall say unto this mountain, Be thou cast down and become smooth, it shall be done. And behold, if ye shall say, that God shall smite this people, it shall come to pass."

These were great blessings. Few men in all the world have received such power as this. Yet it was given to Nephi because of his faithfulness.

Now the Lord gave Nephi a commandment, saying, "I command you that ye shall go and declare unto this people, that thus saith the Lord God, who is the Almighty, except ye repent ye shall be smitten, even unto destruction."

Nephi did not go to his own house, but returned to the heart of the city where the multitude was gathered together, and told them of the destruction which would come upon them if they did not change their way of life.

But although the people had seen the miracle in the judgment hall, when Nephi named the murderer of the judge, they still rejected him and would not believe. They tried to take hold of him to put him in prison, but the Spirit of the Lord snatched him away from the angry crowd.

Nephi did not stop preaching. He went from place to place in all the land, delivering the message which the Lord had given him. They would not listen to him anywhere. But the people did begin to argue and fight among themselves, and many were killed as a result.

The fighting continued in many places. Most of the disputes were started by Gadianton robbers, who mingled with the people.

Nephi did not wish to see the people destroyed by the sword. He felt some lesser affliction should come upon them, to humble them, and make them repent. So he prayed to the Lord that a famine might come into the land.

The famine came. For more than two years it lasted, and many died of starvation in the more wicked parts of the land. The famine extended even among the Lamanites. When so many of the Nephites died of starvation, and they began to see that they all might die, they began to remember the words of Nephi. They came to their governors and judges, asking that they go to Nephi and say, "We know that thou art a man of God, and therefore cry unto the Lord our God, that he turn away from us this famine, lest all the words which thou hast spoken concerning our destruction be fulfilled."

The people repented in sackcloth and ashes. They did all they could to show the Lord they were sincere. They even destroyed the band of Gadianton robbers, so that not one was left.

The judges came to Nephi, as the people had asked, pleading with him to pray to the Lord that the famine might end. This he did. Shortly afterward, rain began to fall on the land and the grass grew, the land yielded crops of grain and other foods, and the lives of the people were spared. They praised the Lord, and kept his commandments. They honored Nephi as a true servant of God.

Nephi's brother Lehi was a great help to him, and stood by his side in all his work.

But the repentance of the people did not last. Hardly were the effects of the famine over than they began to go back into their sinful ways. They even formed another band of Gadianton robbers, with all the secret oaths and crimes of the first band.

CHAPTER SEVENTY

Samuel The Lamanite

Helaman 13-16.

*F*IVE YEARS before the birth of Christ, a Lamanite prophet named Samuel was raised up by the Lord. He came among the people of Zarahemla, preaching to them, and calling them to repentance.

Except for the members of the Church, the Nephites were a wicked people. The Lamanites were much more righteous, and many of them belonged to the Church and kept the commandments.

The wicked people of Zarahemla drove Samuel out of their city as he preached repentance to them. Discouraged, he turned and was about to go home to the Lamanites. But the voice of the Lord came to him, commanding him to go again to the city of Zarahemla, and prophesy to them all the things the Lord would put into his mind to say.

When Samuel tried to re-enter the city to preach again as the Lord had told him, the people would not let him come through the gates. So he climbed to the top of the wall surrounding the city, and preached from there. The prophecies he uttered at that time should have frightened the Nephites, but not many believed. He told them three important things:

He said that if the Nephites did not repent, they would be completely destroyed in four hundred years.

He then told them that in five years Jesus would come, and gave them a sign by which they could know when he was born in Bethlehem.

Also he told them that great signs would be shown throughout America at the time of the crucifixion of the Savior.

In telling them about their final destruction Samuel said:

"Because of the hardness of the hearts of the people of the Nephites, except they repent, I will take away my word from them, and I will withdraw my Spirit from them, and I will suffer them no longer, and I will turn the hearts of their brethren against them. And four hundred years shall not pass away before I will cause that they shall be smitten; yea, I will visit them with the sword and with famine, and with pestilence. Yea, I will visit them in my fierce anger, and there shall be those of the fourth generation, who shall live, of your enemies, to behold your utter destruction; and this shall surely come, except ye repent, saith the Lord; and those of the fourth generation shall visit your destruction."

He told them even their great city Zarahemla should be destroyed, as would also the other great and wicked cities of the Nephites.

Then he told of the coming of the Savior. "Behold, I give unto you a sign; for five years more cometh, and behold, then cometh the Son of God to redeem all those who shall believe on his name. And behold, this will I give unto you for a sign at the time of his coming: for behold, there shall be great lights in heaven, insomuch that in the night before he cometh there shall be no darkness, insomuch that it shall appear unto man as if it was day. Therefore there shall be one day and a night, and a day, as if it were one day; and there were no night, and this shall be unto you for a sign; for ye shall know of the rising of the sun, and also of its setting. Therefore there shall be two days and a night; nevertheless the night shall not be darkened; and it shall be the night before he is born.

"And behold, there shall a new star arise, such an one as ye never have beheld; and this also shall be a sign unto you. And behold this is not all; there shall be many signs and wonders in heaven. And it shall come to pass that ye shall all be amazed, and

211

wonder, insomuch that ye shall fall to the earth. And it shall come come to pass that whosoever shall believe on the Son of God, the same shall have everlasting life."

Samuel then gave them a sign by which they could know of the death of the Savior, when he was crucified on Mt. Calvary, in Jerusalem. Before giving them the sign, he told them the meaning of the resurrection, that when Jesus was resurrected, it opened the way for all mankind to be resurrected.

Then he gave them the sign, saying:

"As I said unto you concerning another sign, a sign of his death, behold, in that day that he shall suffer death, the sun shall be darkened and refuse to give his light unto you; and also the moon and the stars; and there shall be no light upon the face of this land, even from the time that he shall suffer death, for the space of three days, to the time that he shall rise again from the dead.

"Yea, at the time that he shall yield up the ghost, there shall be thunderings and lightnings for the space of many hours, and the earth shall shake and tremble, and the rocks which are upon the face of this earth, which are both above the earth and beneath, which ye know at this time are solid, or the more part of it is one solid mass, shall be broken up. Yea, they shall be rent in twain, and shall ever after be found in seams and in cracks, and in broken fragments upon the face of the whole earth; yea, both above the earth and beneath.

"And there shall be great tempests, and there shall be many mountains laid low, like unto a valley, and there shall be many places, which are now called valleys, which shall become mountains, whose height thereof is great. And many highways shall be broken up, and many cities shall become desolate. And many graves shall be opened, and shall yield up many of their dead; and many saints shall appear unto many.

"And behold thus hath the angel spoken unto me; for he said unto me, that there should be thunderings and lightnings for the space of many hours; and he said unto me that while the thunder and lightning lasted, and the tempest, that these things should be, and that darkness should cover the face of the whole earth for the space of three days."

Samuel said that these things would take place so that there would be no excuse for any one on the earth to refuse to believe in God.

As they listened to Samuel, some of the Nephites believed, and asked for baptism. But others were angry, and threw stones and shot arrows at him as he stood on the high wall. But the Lord protected him, and no one could hit him. Seeing this, still others believed that he was a prophet of God, and went to Nephi for baptism.

But the more stubborn still would not believe, and tried to capture Samuel, but he jumped down from the wall, and escaped. He was next heard of preaching to his own people, the Lamanites.

The righteous people were more righteous after this, but the wicked grew more wicked. Angels came to the righteous, preaching to them. But the wicked continued to say there is no Christ.

CHAPTER SEVENTY-ONE

The Sign of Christ's Birth

III Nephi 1.

ABOUT six hundred years after Lehi had left Jerusalem, Nephi the son of Helaman, who had been such a strength to the Church, called to him his eldest son, whose name was also Nephi.

He gave to his son all of the records which had been kept since the coming of the Nephites to the Promised Land, and also entrusted to him the other sacred things which had been in the care of the prophets.

Then Nephi went away from the land. Where he went no one knew. Like Alma and Moses, he disappeared from the earth. His son Nephi then began to keep the records and to labor in the Church as his father had done.

During the next year, many of the prophecies began to be fulfilled. Great miracles were performed by the leaders of the Church, and faith increased.

But the wicked among them began to say that the five years spoken of by Samuel the Lamanite had passed, and that his prophecy had not been fulfilled. These people began to persecute the members of the Church because of their faith.

So severe did the persecutions become, that the unbelievers set a certain day, saying that unless the sign spoken of by Samuel should come to pass by that time, all members of the Church would be put to death.

Nephi was deeply grieved. He knew that Samuel was a true prophet, and he knew that Jesus would come. He went out alone and prayed to the Lord in behalf of his people, that they might not be killed because they believed in the words of Samuel. He prayed all day long, and then the voice of the Lord came to him, saying:

"Lift up your head and be of good cheer, for behold, the time is at hand, and on this night shall the sign be given, and on the morrow come I into the world, to show unto the world that I will fulfill all that which I have caused to be spoken by the mouth of my holy prophets.

"Behold, I come unto my own, to fulfill all things which I have made known unto the children of men, from the foundation of the world, and do the will, both of the Father, and of the Son— of the Father, because of me, and of the Son, because of my flesh. And behold, the time is at hand, and this night shall the sign be given."

That night as the sun went down, no darkness came. Every-one was surprised. Many who had not believed the words of the prophet fell to the earth in great fear as they remembered what they had threatened to do to the faithful believers in the Lord. They thought of what the prophets had said, and began to fear greatly because of their own iniquity.

Throughout the night the light remained, just as bright as at noonday. The next morning the people saw the sun come up as usual, and they knew that this was the day on which the Lord was to be born in Bethlehem.

Then a new star appeared in the heavens, as Samuel had told them, and it shone with great brilliance. It too proved the truth of all the prophecies, and also that Jesus was born.

Many people were converted by these signs, and came to Nephi for baptism.

CHAPTER SEVENTY-TWO

White Lamanites

III Nephi 2 and 3.

*T*HE REPENTANCE of the Nephites following the sign of Christs's coming did not last long. The young people, who at the time of the sign, were too young to understand what it meant, rebelled against the truth, and began to sin in many ways.

As they grew older they formed robber bands which afflicted both the Nephites and the Lamanites. These robber bands called themselves after Gadianton, once more, and became so numerous that they formed armies which attacked cities and laid waste farm lands.

To protect themselves from these attacks, all of the Lamanites who had joined the Church joined with the Nephite Saints. They organized an army of their own to defend themselves against the Gadianton robbers, and to preserve their right to freedom of religion for the persecution against them was great.

The Lord was mindful of these Lamanite Saints, and when they proved their faithfulness, and came to live with the Nephites, the Lord took from them the curse of the black skin, and their skin became white, like the Nephites'. Their young men were handsome, and their daughters very fair, and from then on they were known as Nephites. This great blessing took place during the thirteenth year after the birth of the Savior.

During the next year, a large army of Nephites went in search of the robbers and drove them back into the mountains, where they hid in secret places. They remained in hiding about a year, and then came again. Because there were so many wicked people among the Nephites, the robbers gained power over them, and many of them joined the robber bands.

In the sixteenth year after the birth of the Savior, the governor of the land received a letter from the robber chief demanding that the Nephites surrender to him, and threatening to kill all of the Nephites if they refused to do so.

The governor was surprised at the boldness of the robber chief, but the governor was a good man, and was not easily frightened. He did not reply to the letter, but asked all of the Nephites to call upon the Lord for protection, and for strength to resist the attack.

He sent a proclamation throughout the land, telling the people to gather into one central place, bringing their flocks and herds, and anything else of value. Then he had fortifications built around this place, and put soldiers on guard.

The governor also preached to his people, and told them that unless they were willing to repent, they could not expect to be spared in the coming attack. With such power did he speak, that the people were impressed, and they all did as the governor directed.

One of the Nephite prophets, Gidgiddoni was appointed commander of the army. Some of the people asked him to attack the robbers where they were, but the general preferred to wait behind their fortifications until they were attacked.

The place where the people were gathered together was the land where the cities of Zarahemla and Bountiful were. The people gathered by the tens of thousands. Not only did the people help prepare for their defense, but they repented of their sins and prayed continually to the Lord.

Having built their forts, and made weapons of every kind known the them, the repentant Nephites now waited for the attack.

CHAPTER SEVENTY-THREE

The Robbers Defeated

III Nephi 4.

*T*HE ARMIES of the Gadianton robbers were numbered in the tens of thousands. They were evil people, who loved crime. They looked very much like the Lamanites before their conversion to the Church. Their heads were shaved, they wore no clothes except a lamb-skin draped around their hips. They did not work for a living, but plundered their neighbors and stole whatever they could. Wild game was plentiful, and they were good hunters.

When the Nephites refused to surrender to them, they decided to attack the Nephite cities and rob them of food and valuables. But when they came into the Nephite lands, they found their cities had been abandoned, and the Nephites were all gathered together in one place for defense.

The robbers thought they would be able to get food from the Nephite cities, but there was none there. The Nephites had taken all their food and other supplies with them. So the robbers had to go back into the wilderness to kill wild animals for their living.

It took so much game to feed such a large army, that it was not long before all of the animals good for food had been killed. Then the robbers began to be hungry. They held a council of war, and decided that they must attack the Nephites or starve.

When the Nephites saw how fierce they looked as they approached they bowed down before the Lord in prayer, asking him to strengthen them in battle. The robbers thought the Nephites had fallen down from fear, and were confident of having an easy victory.

But the Lord heard the prayer of the Nephites and strength-ened them. The robbers rushed at them, but the Nephites were ready. The battle was so fierce that more men were killed at that time than in any battle since Lehi left Jerusalem.

The robbers were completely defeated. They ran for their lives, but the Nephites followed them, and killed every one they caught.

Among those killed was the robber leader, whose name was Giddianhi. He was wearied by the long fight, and so tired from running for safety that the Nephites easily caught up with him and killed him.

The Nephites drove the remaining robbers into the wilderness, and then returned to protect their own cities and families.

They had peace for two years afterward, but then the robbers came once more, determined to steal food and supplies from the Nephites. They believed that the best way to conquer them was to lay siege to the large city in which all of the Nephites were gathered. They believed that if they surrounded the city, and kept the Nephites from coming out to farm their land, they could starve them into submission.

They did not know that the Nephites, when they decided to gather into this place, had brought with them enough food to last for seven years. Their leaders knew that the fight with the robbers would last a long time, and felt that a seven years' supply would be enough.

The robbers began a siege of the city. They waited, thinking that the Nephites would have to give up. But the longer the siege lasted, the worse became the plight of the robbers, for they were the ones who were without food. They could not find enough game in the nearby wilderness to feed them, and they would not work. Hunger was now their worst enemy.

The Nephites, learning of this, began sending their armies out at night to attack the hungry robbers who were surrounding their city. Many of the outlaws were killed in these night attacks. Then the Nephites sent out soldiers in the daytime, to attack the robbers, who were by this time so hungry they could not fight well. At last their hunger became so intense and the attacks by the Nephites so severe, that the robbers believed they should end the siege. Their new leader, Zemnarihah ordered them to begin to march homeward.

The Nephites learned of this through their spies, and during the night sent one of their armies ahead of the robbers, to surprise them and cut them off. Then they sent a second army, so that next day, when the first army attacked the robbers from the front, the second one could fight them from the rear.

When the robbers saw they were caught between two Nephite armies, they became very frightened. Many gave up their arms and became prisoners of the Nephites, and all the others were killed.

The bandit leader, Zemnarihah, was taken prisoner also, and hanged from the top of a tree.

When this battle was over, and all the robbers had been killed or taken prisoner, the Nephites thanked the Lord for giving them the victory. They sang songs praising his name. Their hearts were filled with joy, and many of the soldiers wept in gratitude to the Lord for delivering them from the robbers, and helping them to establish peace in the land once more.

CHAPTER SEVENTY-FOUR

Deeds of Darkness

III Nephi 6 and 7.

*H*AVING beaten the Gadianton robbers in battle, the Nephites left their fortress and returned home. They had not yet eaten all of the food which they had taken with them when the robbers forced them to fortify themselves. And they still had all their precious possessions which the robbers had tried to take from them.

As they planted their farms, they decided that the robbers whom they had captured must also be made to work. They gave them some land and made them till it. These robbers had entered into a covenant of peace with the Nephites in order to avoid being killed, and still fearing for their lives, they now did as they were told.

With the return of peace, the Nephites were able to work and provide for themselves the things which they needed. It was not long before they were wealthy again, and then became proud. Many of them quickly forgot that the Lord had so recently strengthened them so that they could defeat the robber armies. When these people saw the faithful members of the Church serving the Lord, they began to persecute them. Wickedness increased among them.

Prophets came among the people warning them once more that they would be punished severely if they did not repent. The wicked people and some of the evil officials and judges arrested the prophets, and put them to death.

It was against the law to put a person to death without permission of the governor. But the wicked judges killed the prophets secretly, not reporting it until after the execution had taken place.

When the governor heard of it, he had one guilty judge arrested, and prepared to hold a trial for him. But this judge had

221

many friends and relatives, who came to his aid. Some of the judges who were opposed to the Church and had been angry at the prophets, were in sympathy with the accused judge. They and the relatives of the judge met together and plotted to free their friend.

This judge was considered guilty of murder, for having killed the prophets. But his friends were so wicked they did not care for the law nor for righteousness. All they wanted was to save his life.

They gathered many others about them, and planned to do several things: Free their friend, persecute the Saints, and over- throw the governor and appoint a king to rule in his place.

This was a bold scheme. To keep their plans secret they made covenants with each other, like the oaths of the Gadianton rob- bers. Then one of their number secretly murdered the chief judge. When this was done, others of the group led a rebellion which overthrew the government.

Many people now joined this group of rebels. Jacob was one of their leaders. When the government was destroyed, and the chief judge had been killed, they appointed Jacob to be king over the land.

Jacob tried to compel all of the people to accept him. Most of the people were wicked, but still desired a free government, and did not want a king. They joined with the members of the Church in fighting against the "king-men" as they were sometimes called. Jacob soon saw that there were more people against him than there were for him, so he led them out of the land to a secret place, where he planned to wait until all of the traitors among the Nephites joined him.

The people in Zarahemla continued in their wickedness. They still persecuted the Saints, and stoned to death the prophets who came among them.

In spite of these conditions, Nephi, the leader of the Church, kept on with his work. He had been visited by angels, and the Lord himself spoke to him. As he went about preaching the gospel, he performed many great miracles, healing the sick, casting out devils, and when his brother was stoned to death by an angry mob, he raised him from the dead.

The people who were healed by these miracles, faithfully followed Nephi. They were baptized into the Church and began to keep the commandments of the Lord. But the wicked were not converted and continued to persecute the Saints and oppress the poor.

CHAPTER SEVENTY-FIVE

Signs of Christ's Death

III Nephi 8.

*I*N THE fourth day of the first month of the thirty-fourth year after the birth of Jesus, the signs of his death appeared in America.

Samuel the Lamanite had described them when he preached from the walls of Zarahemla. The faithful Saints had been looking forward to seeing them, although the wicked said the signs would never come.

The first sign was a great storm through all Zarahemla. The thunder was so loud it shook the earth. The lightning was more vivid than anyone in the land could remember. The great city of Zarahemla took fire, and burned.

Great earthquakes shook the land. The sea came in and flooded large areas. The city of Moroni sank into the earth, and the sea came in upon it drowning all who lived there.

Earth fell on the city of Moronihah, covering the city and replacing it with a high mountain peak. Although there was great destruction in the land southward, it was worse in the land northward, for there the whole face of the land was changed. Highways were broken up, level roads were spoiled, smooth places became rough.

Many important Nephite cities sank into the earth or were covered with water, and others were burned or shaken down by the earthquakes. Many people lost their lives. Some cities although not destroyed, were badly damaged. The winds were so strong that they carried people away, and they were never heard of again.

Great rocks were broken in pieces; seams and cracks opened in the ground. The strata of the earth were broken up and turned on edge.

224

SIGNS OF CHRIST'S DEATH.

This destruction lasted for three hours, and then suddenly darkness came upon the whole face of the land. It was so thick that people could feel what seemed to be heavy vapor covering the earth. The vapor was so dense that the people could not make a light nor start a fire.

There was no sign of light anywhere, the sun did not shine, nor did the moon or stars. This darkness lasted for three days.

The people were badly frightened. They wept and mourned because of the destruction which had come, and some of them cried out and said, "O that we had repented before this great and terrible day, and then would our brethren have been spared, and they would not have been burned in that great city Zarahemla."

Others said, "O that we had repented before this great and terrible day, and had not killed and stoned the prophets and cast them out. Then would our mothers and our fair daughters and our children have been spared, and not have been buried up in that great city Moronihah."

The Book of Mormon says, "And thus were the howlings of the people great and terrible."

225

CHAPTER SEVENTY-SIX

The Savior Speaks

III Nephi 9 and 10.

*I*N THE SILENCE that followed the terrible storm which swept America at the time of the death of the Savior, a voice was heard. All who had not been killed in the storm or earthquakes, heard it. It began by saying, "Wo, wo, wo unto this people, wo unto the inhabitants of the whole earth, except they shall repent; for the devil laugheth, and his angels rejoice, because of the slain of the fair sons and daughters of my people; and it is because of their iniquity and abominations that they are fallen."

Then the voice described much of the destruction:

"Behold that great city Zarahemla have I burned with fire, and the inhabitants thereof. And behold, that great city Moroni have I caused to be sunk in the depths of the sea, and the inhabitants thereof to be drowned.

"And behold, that great city Moronihah have I covered with earth, and the inhabitants thereof, to hide their iniquities and their abominations from before my face, that the blood of the prophets and the saints shall not come any more unto me against them.

"And behold, the city of Gilgal have I caused to be sunk, and the inhabitants thereof to be buried up in the depths of the earth.

"Yea, and the city of Onihah, and the inhabitants thereof, and the city of Mocum, and the inhabitants thereof, and the city of Jerusalem (one which had been built in America by the Nephites) and the inhabitants thereof; and waters have I caused to come up in the stead thereof, to hide their wickedness and abominations from before my face, that the blood of the prophets and the saints shall not come up any more unto me against them.

226

"And behold, the city of Gadiandi, and the city of Gadiomnah, and the city of Jacob, and the city of Gimgimno, all these have I caused to be sunk, and made hills and valleys in the places thereof; and the inhabitants thereof have I buried up in the depths of the earth, to hide their wickedness and abominations from before my face, that the blood of the prophets and the saints should not come up any more unto me against them.

"And behold, that great city Jacobugath, which was inhabited by the people of King Jacob, have I caused to be burned with fire because of their sins and their wickedness, which was above all the wickedness of the whole earth, because of their secret murders and combinations; for it was they that did destroy the peace of my people and the government of the land; therefore I did cause them to be burned, to destroy them from before my face, that the blood of the prophets and the saints should not come up unto me any more against them.

"And behold the city of Laman, and the city of Josh, and the city of Gad, and the city of Kishkumen, have I caused to be burned with fire, and the inhabitants thereof, because of their wickedness in casting out the prophets, and stoning those whom I did send to declare unto them concerning their wickedness and their abominations.

"And because they did cast them all out, that there were none righteous among them, I did send down fire and destroy them, that their wickedness and abominations might be hid from before my face, that the blood of the prophets and the saints whom I sent among them might not cry unto me from the ground against them.

"And many great destructions have I caused to come upon this land, and upon this people, because of their wickedness and their abominations. O all ye that are spared because ye were more righteous than they, will ye not now return unto me, and repent of your sins, and be converted, that I may heal you?

"Yea, verily I say unto you, if ye will come unto me ye shall have eternal life. Behold, mine arm of mercy is extended towards you, and whosoever will come, him will I receive; and blessed are those who come unto me.

"Behold, I am Jesus Christ, the Son of God. I created the heavens and the earth, and all things that in them are. I was with the Father from the beginning. I am in the Father, and the Father in me; and in me hath the Father glorified his name.

"I came unto my own, and my own received me not. And the scriptures concerning my coming are fulfilled."

Again he appealed to them to repent. He told them of the need to be baptized, and said he came to bring redemption to the world, to save the world from sin.

"Therefore," he said, "whoso repenteth and cometh unto me as a little child, him will I receive, for of such is the kingdom of God. Behold, for such I have laid down my life, and have taken it up again; therefore repent, and come unto me ye ends of the earth, and be saved."

Everyone heard the voice. After the Lord had stopped speaking, there was silence again for many hours. The people were so surprised at the voice, that they stopped their mourning and crying, and waited.

After a long silence, the voice was heard again.

"O ye people of these great cities which have fallen, who are descendants of Jacob, yea, who are of the house of Israel, how oft have I gathered you as a hen gathereth her chickens under her wings, and have nourished you."

Then, to those who had been spared from the destruction he said, "O ye house of Israel whom I have spared, how oft will I gather you as a hen gathereth her chickens under her wings, if ye will repent and return unto me with full purpose of heart."

He was willing to give them another opportunity to repent and come to him, and be blessed, if they would put aside their

228

selfishness and their sins. But if they would not, more destruction would come upon them, for he said, "But if not, O house of Israel, the places of your dwellings shall become desolate until the time of the fulfilling of the covenant to your fathers."

After hearing this, the people began to mourn once more, crying aloud for their loved ones who had died in their homes as the Lord poured out destruction upon them for their wickedness.

CHAPTER SEVENTY-SEVEN

The Terror Ends

III Nephi 10 and 11.

*F*OR THREE DAYS the darkness and terror continued in America. Every word of the prophecy of Samuel the Lamanite was fulfilled. The signs of the death of Jesus on the cross in Jerusalem were seen by all the people.

Nowhere could a light be started, and no one could make a fire. The misty darkness was so heavy that the people could do nothing to pierce it. They knew of the destruction, for the voice of the Lord had told them. They could hear the groanings in the earth, as the rocks split and as great crevasses opened in the ground. They could feel the continual earthquakes. And they did not know what would happen next.

Samuel the Lamanite had told them the darkness and destruction would last for three days. With no sun to shine, and no moon or stars to shed their light at night, it was hard for them to tell when a day was over. They waited, sometimes in silence, sometimes in mourning, knowing that at the end of three days the light would come again.

At last the darkness disappeared. It was morning when the light was seen. The earthquakes were still; no more rocks were broken, and the great openings in the ground closed as the earth came together again.

With the return of the light, the people who were spared stopped weeping. Their mourning was turned to joy as they found so many alive, and they began to thank the Lord for his protection when so many others had lost their lives.

Only the more righteous part of the people had been spared. The wicked ones had been killed as their cities were burned, or buried by mountains falling on them, or flooded by the sea.

With the return of light, the people who had heard the voice of the Lord and had waited so long and fearfully for the end of the destruction, went out of their homes to see what had happened.

The many changes which had taken place in the appearance of the land astonished them. Mountains had been flattened, and where there had been valleys, mountains now appeared. There were new lakes and arms of the sea. Great sections of rock which had been flat and hidden in the earth, now protruded so that they stood on edge.

People spoke to each other about the prophecies of the Lord telling of the death of the Savior and the signs which should accompany it. They remembered Samuel the Lamanite and his predictions, and knew that they had all been fulfilled.

It was a strange and greatly changed world in which they now lived.

CHAPTER SEVENTY-EIGHT

The Savior Appears

III Nephi 11.

*M*ANY righeous people had lived in the land called Bountiful. They were spared during the three days of darkness and destruction. When the light returned they went to where their temple stood, and there saw the many changes which had taken place in the land.

As they stood talking with each other, they heard a voice as if it were speaking from heaven. It was not a loud voice, neither was it harsh. It was soft, but it pierced the hearts of all who were there, frightening them so that they trembled. It caused their hearts to burn within them, but they could not understand the words spoken. It seemed to be a strange language.

As they wondered what it meant, the voice came again, but still they could not understand the words that were spoken. They looked up toward the sky in the direction from which the voice seemed to come, and listened intently.

A third time the voice came. Now they could understand the words. It was the voice of God, which said, "Behold my Beloved Son, in whom I am well pleased, in whom I have glorified my name—hear ye him."

As they looked into the sky and listened to the voice, they saw a Personage descending from heaven, dressed in a white robe. He came down and stood in the midst of the people who were near the temple. They all looked at him, but none dared to speak.

The glorious Personage then reached out his hand, and began to speak to the people. His first words told them who he was:

"Behold, I am Jesus Christ, whom the prophets testified shall come into the world. And behold, I am the light and the life of the world; and I have drunk out of that bitter cup which the Father hath given me, and have glorified the Father in taking upon me the sins of the world, in the which I have suffered the will of the Father in all things from the beginning."

The people remembered that the prophets had told them that Jesus would show himself to them after his resurrection. They now understood the words of the Father, as he introduced his Beloved Son to them: "Behold my Beloved Son, in whom I am well pleased, in whom I have glorified my name —hear ye him."

As Jesus told them who he was the multitude fell down before him, and worshipped him. To dispel any doubts in their minds about him, he called them to him, and said:

"Arise and come forth unto me, that ye may thrust your hands into my side, and also that ye may feel the prints of the nails in my hands and in my feet, that ye may know that I am the God of Israel, and the God of the whole earth, and have been slain for the sins of the world."

The people then did as he told them. They came one by one, and thrust their hands into his side, and felt the prints of the nails in his hands and feet, and as the scriptures say, "this they did do, going forth one by one until they had all gone forth, and did see with their eyes and did feel with their hands, and did know of a surety and did bear record, that it was he, of whom it was written by the prophets, that should come."

When all had gone up and seen and felt him they cried aloud saying, "Hosanna! Blessed be the name of the Most High God!"

Then they all fell down before his feet, and worshipped him. There were there twenty-five hundred people, men, women and children, and they all both saw and touched the resurrected Savior.

CHAPTER SEVENTY-NINE

Twelve Disciples Called

III Nephi 11 and 12; I Nephi 12:8-9; Moroni 2:1-3.

*N*EPHI, the prophet who had labored among the people before the destruction came upon them, was among those who were present near the temple when Jesus appeared among the Nephites. He had testified boldly to the wicked about the Savior, and had borne testimony to them that Jesus did live. Angels had visited him at that time to help him in his ministry.

The Savior knew Nephi was among those who had gathered there as he descended from the skies. He called for him to come forward from among the rest of the people. As Nephi came, he bowed down before Jesus and kissed his feet. The Lord commanded him to arise. He did so, and stood before the Savior, waiting his command.

Jesus said to him, "I give unto you power that ye shall baptize this people when I am again ascended into heaven."

Then he called eleven others and gave them the same power, telling them how to perform baptisms. He said, "Whoso repenteth of his sins through your words and desireth to be baptized in my name, on this wise shall ye baptize them—Behold, ye shall go down and stand in the water, and in my name shall ye baptize them. And now behold, these are the words which ye shall say, calling them by name, saying: Having authority given me of Jesus Christ, I baptize you in the name of the Father, and of the Son, and of the Holy Ghost. Amen. And then shall ye immerse them in the water, and come forth again out of the water."

The Savior told them that they must perform all baptisms in this way, and that there should be no arguments about it. He taught them to avoid disputes about any phase of his doctrine,

Nephi bows before Jesus

and said, "There shall be no disputations among you, as there have hitherto been; neither shall there be disputations among you concerning the points of my doctrine, as there have hitherto been. For verily, verily I say unto you, he that hath the spirit of contention is not of me, but is of the devil, who is the father of contention, and he stirreth up the hearts of men to contend with anger, one with another. Behold, this is not my doctrine, to stir up the hearts of men with anger, one against another; but this is my doctrine, that such things should be done away."

He then explained that all who were baptized and lived the gospel will be saved. He taught them that those who do not accept the gospel, but reject baptism will not be saved.

To those who would believe and accept baptism by immersion in water, he promised the gift of the Holy Ghost.

But, he said, "ye must repent, and become as a little child, and be baptized in my name, or ye can in no wise receive these things."

Having chosen his twelve Nephite disciples, and instructed them how to baptize, Jesus again turned to the multitude, and said:

"Blessed are ye if ye shall give heed unto the words of these twelve whom I have chosen from among you to minister unto you, and to be your servants; and unto them I have given power that they may baptize you with water; and after that ye are baptized with water, behold, I will baptize you with fire and with the Holy Ghost; therefore blessed are ye if ye shall believe in me and be baptized, after that ye have seen me and know that I am."

The twelve Nephite disciples were ordained by the Lord, who laid his hands upon their heads, and said, calling each one by name:

"Ye shall call on the Father in my name, in mighty prayer; and after ye have done this ye shall have power that to him upon whom ye shall lay your hands, ye shall give the Holy Ghost; and in my name shall ye give it, for thus do mine apostles."

These twelve men had been shown in vision to the first Nephi, son of Lehi. The angel who explained the vision to Nephi at that time, said "Behold the twelve disciples of the Lamb, who are chosen to minister unto thy seed. Thou rememberest the twelve apostles of the Lamb? (referring to the twelve chosen in Palestine). Behold they are they who shall judge the twelve tribes of Israel; wherefore, the twelve ministers of thy seed shall be judged of them; for ye are of the house of Israel. And these twelve ministers whom thou beholdest shall judge thy seed. And behold, they are righteous forever; for because of their faith in the Lamb of God their garments are made white in his blood."

These twelve ministers, or disciples, as they were called among the Nephites, performed a great work. More will be told of the miracles they performed and of their labors among the people.

CHAPTER EIGHTY

The Savior's Sermon

III Nephi 12-16.

ONE OF THE greatest sermons ever given is known in the Bible as the Sermon on the Mount. When Jesus came among the Nephites, he gave to them many of the same teachings which appear in that great sermon.

Among the many beautiful things in it are these:

"Blessed are the poor in spirit who come unto me, for theirs is the kingdom of heaven.

"And again, blessed are all they that mourn, for they shall be comforted.

"And blessed are the meek, for they shall inherit the earth.

"And blessed are all they who do hunger and thirst after righteousness, for they shall be filled with the Holy Ghost.

"And blessed are the merciful, for they shall obtain mercy.

"And blessed are all the pure in heart, for they shall see God.

"And blessed are all the peacemakers, for they shall be called the children of God.

"And blessed are all they who are persecuted for my name's sake, for theirs is the kingdom of heaven.

"And blessed are ye when men shall revile you and persecute and shall say all manner of evil against you falsely, for my sake; for ye shall have great joy and be exceeding glad, for great shall be your reward in heaven; for so persecuted they the prophets who were before you."

The Nephites had been living the Law of Moses, which they brought with them when Lehi left Jerusalem. Jesus now told them that he had fulfilled that law, and he gave to them the higher laws of the gospel. The Law of Moses had taught them that if they should harm another person, they should suffer the same harm themselves, "an eye for an eye and a tooth for a tooth." But the law of the gospel which the Lord now gave taught them to do unto others as they would have others do unto them; to love their neighbors as themselves, to be forgiving and kind.

He said, "Therefore, if ye shall come unto me, or shall desire to come unto me, and rememberest that thy brother hath aught against thee—go thy way unto thy brother, and first be reconciled to thy brother, and then come unto me with full purpose of heart, and I will receive you."

He said, "Behold, it is written, an eye for an eye, and a tooth for a tooth; but I say unto you, that ye shall not resist evil, but whosoever shall smite thee on thy right cheek, turn to him the other also; and if any man will sue thee at the law and take away thy coat, let him have thy cloak also; and whosoever shall compel thee to go a mile, go with him twain."

Another of his teachings, given this first day among the Nephites was this:

"Give to him that asketh thee, and from him that would borrow of thee, turn thou not away. And behold it is written also, that thou shalt love thy neighbor and hate thine enemy; but behold I say unto you, love your enemies, bless them that curse you, do good to them that hate you, and pray for them who despitefully use you and persecute you; that you may be the children of your Father who is in heaven; for he maketh his sun to rise on the evil and on the good."

He told them not to judge their neighbors, for, he said, "with what judgment ye judge, ye shall be judged; and with what measure ye mete, it shall be measured to you again. And why beholdest thou the mote that is in thy brother's eye, but considerest not the beam that is in thine own eye?" He taught "first cast the beam out of thine own eye! and then shalt thou see clearly to cast the mote out of thy brother's eye.''

He told them to beware of false prophets and false teachers, who would come among them like wolves in sheep's clothing. He said they could tell these persons by their fruits, for a good tree brings forth good fruit, but a bad tree will bring forth bad fruit.

CHAPTER EIGHTY-ONE

The Lord's Prayer

III Nephi 13-15.

Our way of communicating with the Lord is through prayer. Jesus has always taught his people to pray, and to pray often. In his first great sermon to the Nephites, he taught them the importance of simple, humble prayer.

He does not approve prayers which are made to impress other people.

"When thou prayest," he said, "thou shalt not do as the hypocrites, for they love to pray, standing in the synagogues and in the corners of the streets, that they may be seen of men. Verily I say unto you, they have their reward.

"But thou, when thou prayest, enter into thy closet, and when thou hast shut thy door, pray to thy Father who is in secret; and thy Father, who seeth in secret, shall reward thee openly.

"But when ye pray, use not vain repetitions, as the heathen, for they think that they shall be heard for their much speaking. Be not ye therefore like unto them, for your Father knoweth what things ye have need of before ye ask him."

Then he gave a pattern for their prayers. He said:

"After this manner therefore pray ye:

"Our Father who art in heaven, hallowed be thy name. Thy will be done on earth as it is in heaven.

"And forgive us our debts, as we forgive our debtors.

"And lead us not into temptation, but deliver us from evil.

"For thine is the kingdom, and the power, and the glory, forever. Amen."

He encouraged the people to ask for the things they need. "Ask," he said, "and it shall be given unto you; seek, and ye shall find; knock, and it shall be opened unto you. For everyone that asketh, receiveth; and he that seeketh, findeth; and to him that knocketh, it shall be opened. Or what man is there of you, who, if his son ask bread, will give him a stone? Or if he ask a fish, will he give him a serpent? If ye then, being evil, know how to give good gifts unto your children, how much more shall your Father who is in heaven give good things to them that ask him?"

But to obtain blessings from the Lord in prayer, we must do what he tells us. We must obey him, for he said, "Not every one that saith unto me, Lord, Lord, shall enter into the kingdom of heaven; but he that doeth the will of my Father who is in heaven."

He taught that we cannot live in sin, and still profess to serve the Lord. "No man can serve two masters; for either he will hate the one and love the other, or else he will hold to the one and despise the other. Ye cannot serve God and Mammon."

He spoke again of the hypocrites, whom he dispised, and urged his people to avoid their examples. "When ye fast," he continued, "be not as the hypocrites, of a sad countenance, for they disfigure their faces that they may appear unto men to fast. Verily, I say unto you, they have their reward. But thou, when thou fastest, anoint thy head, and wash thy face; that thou appear not unto men to fast, but unto thy Father, who is in secret; and thy Father, who seeth in secret, shall reward thee openly."

Then, turning from the multitude for a moment, he spoke directly to his twelve ministers, or disciples, and told them they must not worry about how they would support themselves in the ministry, for the Lord would take care of them.

"Therefore," he said, "I say unto you, take no thought for your life, what ye shall eat, or what ye shall drink; nor yet for your body, what ye shall put on. Is not the life more than meat, and the body than raiment? Behold the fowls of the air, for they sow not, neither do they reap nor gather into barns; yet your heavenly Father feedeth them. Are ye not much better than they?

"And why take ye thought for raiment? Consider the lilies of the field, how they grow; they toil not, neither do they spin; and yet I say unto you, that even Solomon, in all his glory, was not arrayed like one of these. Wherefore, if God so clothe the grass of the field, which today is, and tomorrow is cast into the oven, even so will he clothe you, if ye are not of little faith.

"Therefore take no thought, saying, What shall we eat? or, What shall we drink? or, Wherewithal shall we be clothed? For your heavenly Father knoweth that ye have need of all these things.

"But seek ye first the kingdom of God and his righteousness, and all these things shall be added unto you."

The Savior held up to the Nephites, as he had to the Jews, the ideal of becoming like himself, and like his Father in Heaven. In preaching this doctrine to the Nephites he said:

"I would that ye should be perfect even as I, or your Father who is in heaven is perfect."

CHAPTER EIGHTY-TWO

Jesus The Lawgiver

III Nephi 15.

*A*S JESUS taught the Nephites the great principles of the gospel, and told them that they were to follow these teachings and no longer observe the Law of Moses, he saw that many in the multitude did not understand.

All their lives they had been taught the Law of Moses. It had been brought from Jerusalem by Lehi and his sons, and was written on the brass plates they had obtained from Laban. All through the centuries the Nephites had taught their children to observe this law.

They did not remember that in the days of Moses the people once had the gospel, but because of their sins, it was taken from them. The Law of Moses was given to the ancient Israelites in its place. It was to be a "schoolmaster" to teach them obedience, so that in some future time they would be able to live the fulness of the gospel. Jesus now was bringing them this fulness, and for that reason, the "schoolmaster," or Law of Moses, was no longer needed.

Seeing that they were puzzled about this, Jesus said, "Marvel not that I said unto you that old things had passed away, and that all things had become new. Behold, I say unto you that the law is fulfilled that was given unto Moses."

In making this explanation, he told them another truth:

"Behold, I am he that gave the law, and I am he who covenanted with my people Israel; therefore, the law in me is fulfilled, for I have come to fulfil the law; therefore it hath an end."

Jesus, whose name is also Jehovah, was the God of the Old Testament who gave the law to Moses when ancient Israel traveled in the wilderness. It was he who spoke to Moses at Mt. Sinai. Since he had given the law, he could decide it was no longer needed. And this he did.

"Behold," he continued, "I do not destroy the prophets (meaning the teachings of the prophets), for as many as have not been fulfilled in me, verily I say unto you, shall all be fulfilled. And because I said unto you that old things have passed away, I do not destroy that which hath been spoken concerning things which are to come. For behold, the covenant which I have made with my people is not all fulfilled; but the law which was given unto Moses hath an end in me."

He announced himself again as the law-giver. "Behold, I am the law, and the light. Look unto me, and endure to the end, and ye shall live; for unto him that endureth to the end will I give eternal life. Behold, I have given unto you the commandments; therefore keep my commandments. And this is the law and the prophets, for they truly testified of me."

Turning again from the multitude, and speaking only to his twelve ministers, he said, "Ye are my disciples; and ye are a light unto this people, who are a remnant of the house of Joseph. And behold, this is the land of your inheritance; and the Father hath given it unto you."

Then he told them that he had "other sheep," some in Jerusalem, and others whom the Father had led away. The Nephites themselves were some of those "other sheep." He had so spoken of them while he was yet in Jerusalem.

He said that the gospel would some time be given to the Gentile nations, but that the Gentiles would not be blessed with his personal ministry, as were the Nephites and Jews. To the Gentiles he would manifest himself only by the Holy Ghost.

But, he said to the Nephites, "ye have both heard my voice, and seen me; and ye are my sheep, and ye are numbered among those whom the Father hath given me."

CHAPTER EIGHTY-THREE

He Blesses the Children

III Nephi 17.

*J*ESUS looked at the people who had gathered about him and listened to his great sermon. He saw that many of them were deeply affected, but that they could not understand all he had said.

"I perceive that ye are weak," he said, "that ye cannot understand all my words which I am commanded of the Father to speak unto you at this time.

"Therefore, go ye unto your homes, and ponder upon the things which I have said, and ask of the Father, in my name, that ye may understand, and prepare your minds for the morrow, and I come unto you again.

"But now I go unto the Father, and also to show myself unto the lost tribes of Israel, for they are not lost unto the Father, for he knoweth whither he hath taken them."

As he looked at the people who did not want to leave him, he saw that they were in tears and were hoping that he would remain with them. His own soul was filled with mercy. He wished to bless them. So he said:

"Have ye any that are sick among you? Bring them hither. Have ye any that are lame, or blind, or halt, or maimed, or leprous, or that are withered, or that are deaf, or that are afflicted in any manner? Bring them hither and I will heal them, for I have compassion upon you."

He saw that they desired him to bless them as he had those who lived in Jerusalem. And he saw that their faith was sufficient, so that he could heal them.

The people quickly brought to him all their sick, blind, and lame, and all who were in any other way afflicted, and he healed every one of them.

CHRIST BLESSES THE CHILDREN.

Then all who were healed bowed down and worshipped him. Their relatives and friends joined them, and weeping for joy, they kissed his feet. They wept so "that they did bathe his feet with their tears."

Jesus now wanted to bless their children, and commanded that they should be brought to him. All who had little ones brought them and they sat down on the ground around him.

Then he stood in the midst of them, but commanded that the parents should kneel on the ground about him and the children.

Jesus himself kneeled upon the earth and prayed to his Father, and all the multitude heard his words. What he said was so sacred that it could not be written. But the multitude who heard said, "The eye hath never seen, neither hath the ear heard, before, so great and marvelous things as we saw and heard Jesus

247

speak unto the Father; and no tongue can speak, neither can there be written by any man, neither can the hearts of men conceive so great and marvelous things as we both saw and heard Jesus speak; and no one can conceive of the joy which filled our souls at the time we heard him pray for us unto the Father."

As Jesus closed his prayer, he arose from his knees, and told the multitude to arise also. "Blessed are ye because of your faith," he told them, "and now behold, my joy is full."

He too then wept for joy, because of their great faith, and all the people saw it.

Then he took their little children, one by one, and blessed them and prayed to the Father for them. When he had finished, he wept again before the multitude.

"Behold your little ones," he said, and as the people looked, they saw the heavens open and angels descended in what appeared to be a blaze of fire. They came down and encircled the children whom Jesus had blessed. The fire came with them, and it too encircled the children, but it was a heavenly fire, and none was burned. The angels then ministered to the children. All the parents saw it, and praised the Lord for his blessings.

CHAPTER EIGHTY-FOUR

The Sacrament Given

III Nephi 18.

STILL LINGERING with the people, Jesus desired one thing more before ascending to his Father, and that was to give to the Nephites the sacrament of the Lord's Supper.

Calling his twelve disciples, he commanded them to bring bread and wine to him. Like the Jews in Palestine, the Nephites made a natural drink from grapes which they called wine.

While the disciples were obtaining the bread and wine, the Savior commanded the multitude to sit upon the earth. Soon the disciples came with their burdens. Jesus took the bread, broke it in pieces, and blessed it. He gave it at first only to his twelve disciples, telling them to eat of it, and after they had eaten, he told them to pass it to the multitude, that all might partake.

After all had been served, Jesus said, "There shall one be ordained among you, and to him will I give power that he shall break bread and bless it and give it unto the people of my Church, unto all those who shall believe and be baptized in my name. And this shall ye always observe to do, even as I have done, even as I have broken bread and blessed it and given it unto you.

"And this shall ye do in remembrance of my body, which I have shown unto you. And it shall be a testimony unto the Father that ye do always remember me. And if ye do always remember me ye shall have my Spirit to be with you."

Having said this, he commanded the disciples to drink of the wine which he blessed, and then pass it to the multitude. When all had partaken the Lord said, "Blessed are ye for this thing which ye have done, for this is fulfilling my commandments, and this doth witness unto the Father that ye are willing to do that which I have commanded you. And this shall ye always do to those who repent and are baptized in my name; and ye shall do it in remembrance of my blood, which I have shed for you, that ye may witness unto the Father that ye do always remember me. And if ye do always remember me ye shall have my Spirit to be with you."

He told them that those who did this were "built upon my rock," but those who did not, "are not built upon my rock, but are built upon a sandy foundation; and when the rain descends, and the floods come, and the winds blow, and beat upon them, they shall fall, and the gates of hell are ready open to receive them.

"Therefore, blessed are ye if ye shall keep my commandments, which the Father hath commanded me that I should give unto you."

The Savior once again taught the people to pray. He had already given them the Lord's Prayer, telling them to pray to the Father in the name of Jesus. Now he desired to tell some of the reasons why they should pray. But first he spoke to his disciples alone.

"Verily, I say unto you," he said, "ye must watch and pray always, lest ye be tempted by the devil, and ye be led away captive by him. And as I have prayed among you even so shall ye pray in my Church, among my people who do repent and are baptized in my name. Behold I am the light; I have set an example for you."

Turning from the disciples, and facing the multitude he told them also that prayer was a way to prevent sin. "Verily, verily I say unto you," he said, "ye must watch and pray always lest ye enter into temptation; for Satan desireth to have you, that he may sift you as wheat. Therefore ye must always pray unto the Father in my name; and whatsoever ye shall ask the Father in my name, which is right, believing that ye shall receive, behold it shall be given unto you."

Jesus knew that family prayer was very important, and he taught the Nephites that they should pray together as families, that all members would be strengthened against temptation. So he said, "Pray in your families unto the Father, always in my name, that your wives and your children may be blessed."

Jesus also taught the Nephites to attend their Church meetings regularly, and to welcome non-members of the Church also, that they might be converted.

"Ye shall not forbid any man from coming unto you when ye shall meet together, but suffer them that they may come unto you and forbid them not; but ye shall pray for them, and shall not cast them out; and if it so be that they come unto you oft ye shall pray for them unto the Father, in my name."

He told them that as he was a light to the world, the members of the Church must also hold up their light to other men.

Having taught the people to welcome strangers to their meetings, he now turned again to the twelve disciples, and impressed upon them once more the sacredness of the sacrament. He told them that they, as his ministers, must not allow any one to partake of the sacrament unworthily. He said that they must pray for the unrepentant, and encourage them to do right, but that they must not allow the wicked to partake of his sacrament. Only those who repent, and are willing to serve the Lord are to partake.

Again he told them to avoid arguments about his teachings, saying, "Blessed are ye if ye have no disputations among you."

At last he told them that the time had come for him to return to his Father. He came to each of the twelve disciples, and put his hands upon them, one by one, and spoke to them as he did so. The multitude could not hear what he said, but the disciples told them afterward that he gave to them the power to give the gift of the Holy Ghost.

After he had given each of the twelve this power, a cloud came down and overshadowed the multitude so that they could not see him. While they were covered by this cloud, the Savior ascended into heaven. Although the multitude did not see him ascend, his twelve disciples did, and bore testimony of it to all the people.

CHAPTER EIGHTY-FIVE

The Disciples Baptized

III Nephi 19.

*T*HE MULTITUDE dispersed after the ascension of Jesus; each family going to their own home.

There were many people who had not heard of the visit of the Savior, and therefore were not present when he came. Those who were there told their friends in other parts of the land, and said that Jesus would come again the next day.

All night long the people gathered from distant places. They too desired to see the Savior, and receive his blessings. There had been two thousand present on the first day. So many gathered for the second day's visit, that the disciples divided them into twelve groups. Each of the disciples stayed with one group, and taught them many of the things which Jesus had told them on the first day's visit. In this way, those who had been absent the day before, learned what had taken place. The disciples were so blessed of the Lord that they repeated word for word the teachings of the Savior.

The twelve disciples were:

Nephi, the great prophet who had labored so hard among the people before the destruction came upon the land.

Nephi's brother, Timothy, whom he raised from the dead after he had been stoned to death by the wicked people who had refused to listen to his teachings.

Nephi's son, Jonas

Mathoni

Mathonihah, brother of Mathoni

Kumen

Kumenonhi

Jeremiah
Shemnon
Jonas
Zedekiah
Isaiah.

Having taught the multitude all the things which Jesus had said the day before, the twelve now knelt together in humble prayer. They asked the Lord for that which they desired most—the holy fire of that Spirit.

After their prayer, they went down to the water's edge, so that each could be baptized. Nephi was first. Then he baptized all the others. When all had received the ordinance, the Holy Ghost came upon them, and they were filled with the power and the holy fire of that Spirit.

The multitudes which were watching the twelve during this time, saw heavenly fire come down from the skies and encircle them. Then angels came down, and ministered to these blessed disciples.

While the angels were ministering to the twelve, Jesus came also, and stood in the midst of them. The Lord turned to the multitude and commanded all the people to kneel upon the ground. He asked his disciples to do likewise, and then he commanded them all to pray. They did so, and in their prayers they called Jesus their Lord and their God.

Jesus walked away by himself, and knelt upon the ground. As he prayed to the Father he said, "Father, I thank thee that thou hast given the Holy Ghost unto these whom I have chosen; and it is because of their belief in me that I have chosen them out of the world. Father, I pray that thou wilt give the Holy Ghost unto all them that shall believe in their words."

Finishing his prayer, the Savior came back to where the disciples were kneeling. He smiled upon them as they prayed there. His face shone with a holy light, and his clothing also. The light was a heavenly white, whiter than anything that had ever been seen on earth. It now rested upon the twelve so that they appeared gloriously white like the Savior. They were purified by the Holy Spirit.

Smiling down upon them, Jesus, said, "Pray on."

Leaving them again, he went a little way off, and knelt down once more and prayed saying, "Father, I thank thee that thou hast purified those whom I have chosen, because of their faith, and I pray for them, and also for them who shall believe on their words, that they may be purified in me, through faith on their words, even as they are purified in me."

He came back to the twelve who were still praying. The heavenly light continued upon them and they were as white and glorious in their appearance as the Savior himself. The Father indeed had purified them, as the Savior had said. Jesus smiled down upon them again.

A third time Jesus went away, and knelt in prayer. This time the multitude could hear what he said, and again his words were so great and sacred that they could not be written.

When he returned to his twelve disciples, he said to them. "So great faith have I never seen among all the Jews; wherefore I could not show unto them so great miracles, because of their unbelief. Verily, I say unto you, there are none of them that have seen so great things as ye have seen; neither have they heard so great things as ye have heard."

CHAPTER EIGHTY-SIX

Another Miracle

III Nephi 20.

*I*N THE second day of his visit among the Nephites, Jesus desired to administer the sacrament once more. Many among the multitude had not been with him on the previous day when he had given the sacrament, and he desired that all who were righteous should receive it.

He now commanded the multitude and his twelve disciples to cease praying and arise. He told them, however, that they should continue to pray in their hearts.

Jesus then took bread, and broke it in pieces and blessed it, and commanded the twelve to pass it to the people. After they had eaten the bread, in remembrance of his body, he blessed their wine and passed it to the twelve, who passed it to the others.

No one had brought either bread or wine to him and they did not know where it came from. But Jesus in a miraculous way caused that both bread and wine be provided, and it was there. He blessed both, and his disciples passed these sacred emblems of his crucifixion among the people.

In Palestine he had miraculously fed five thousand at one time, and four thousand on another occasion when they were hungry. Now among the Nephites he did a similar thing, only instead of feeding them because of their hunger, he provided the bread and wine for the sacrament.

He told all the people that if they would partake of his sacrament worthily, their souls should never hunger nor thirst for spiritual nourishment, for they would always be filled with his spirit.

256

He taught them many things pertaining to their future. He said that in the latter days, the Father would establish a great nation on this American continent, which would be a free country. It would be an instrument in the Lord's hands to help his servants to do their work in the last days in preparation for the second coming of the Savior.

CHAPTER EIGHTY-SEVEN

The Dead Raised

III Nephi 23.

*N*EPHI was the keeper of the records at this time. The Lord desired to have a record kept on the plates of Nephi telling of his appearance and the many great things which had happened since he came among the Nephites.

"Write the things which I have told you," he said, "and according to the time and the will of the Father, they shall go forth unto the Gentiles."

This was a great promise that in times to come the Book of Mormon writings would be brought forth and given to a Gentile people, so that they might believe. Other promises like this were made by the Nephite prophets. We who live today are the Gentile people spoken of, and the Book of Mormon was given to us through the power of the Lord who sent Moroni, as an angel, to Joseph Smith.

Continuing with his promise to the Gentiles to whom the records would be given, Jesus said, "And whosoever will hearken unto my words and repenteth and is baptized, the same shall be saved."

He urged the people to search the scriptures for they would reveal many of his great truths.

Then he told the Nephites that they should write more scriptures of their own, under his guidance. "Behold, other scriptures I would that ye should write, that ye have not."

In all of the excitement of the three days destruction and darkness when no light could be made, Nephi had not done any writing. And during the great events of the last two days, when

Jesus had come among the people, Nephi had not written all that had happened.

Jesus asked to see Nephi's record. When Nephi brought it to him, Jesus read it, and saw that Nephi had not yet written some of the important things which had happened. He said to Nephi, "I commanded my servant Samuel, the Lamanite, that he should testify unto this people, that at the day that the Father should glorify his name in me that there were many saints who should arise from the dead, and should appear unto many, and should minister unto them. Was it not so?"

His twelve disciples remembered, and said, "Yea, Lord, Samuel did prophesy according to thy words, and they were all fulfilled."

Then Jesus asked, "How be it that ye have not written this thing, that many saints did arise and appear unto many and did minister unto them?"

Nephi then remembered that he had not written this event into the record. After the resurrection of Jesus, many of the dead Nephites had arisen from their graves, and had come into the cities and appeared to the people. But Nephi had not put it in his record.

Jesus commanded him that he should write it on the plates, and Nephi obeyed him.

The Savior now met with the little children once more. The spirit of the Lord came upon them, and these little children spoke great prophecies. It was a marvel to all who saw and heard, for the little children spoke the words of God.

The Savior again healed the sick who had come from the more distant places, and had not been present the day before. He raised one man from the dead. He restored the sight of the blind, and those who were deaf were made to hear again. Then he left them, going back to his Father in heaven.

The twelve disciples now began baptizing the people, for they had been converted by the Savior's teachings and miracles, and wished to join his Church. Following their baptism they were filled with the Holy Ghost. More miracles were performed among them by the power of the Lord.

Everyone learned to love his neighbor as himself. They shared their property and their food and had all things in common. There were no poor among them and no rich. All had the same, and they lived together in peace and love, worshipping the Lord and enjoying his blessings.

CHAPTER EIGHTY-EIGHT

The Church Is Named

III Nephi 27.

*A*FTER LABORING among the people, preaching the gospel, and baptizing all the believers, the twelve disciples met together in fasting and prayer.

As they prayed, Jesus came and stood among them and asked, "What will ye that I shall give unto you?"

They said, "Lord, we will that thou wouldst tell us the name whereby we shall call this Church; for there are disputations among the people concerning this matter."

Jesus had already told them that there should be no disputes among them and that they should avoid arguments of all kinds. So he said, "Why is it that the people should murmur and dispute because of this thing? Have they not read the scriptures, which say ye must take upon you the name of Christ, which is my name? For by this name shall ye be called at the last day; and whoso taketh upon him my name, and endureth to the end, the same shall be saved at the last day.

"Therefore," he continued, "whatsoever ye shall do, ye shall do it in my name; therefore ye shall call the Church in my name; and ye shall call upon the Father in my name that he will bless the Church for my sake."

Explaining further he said, "And how be it my Church save it be called in my name? For if a church be called in Moses' name then it be Moses' church; or if it be called in the name of a man then it be the church of a man; but if it be called in my name then it is my church, if it so be that they are built upon my gospel. Verily I say unto you, that ye are built upon my gospel, therefore ye shall call whatsoever things ye do call, in my name;

261

therefore if ye call upon the Father, for the Church, if it be in my name the Father will hear you.

"And if it so be that the Church is built upon my gospel then will the Father show forth his own works in it. But if it be not built upon my gospel, and is built upon the works of men, or upon the works of the devil, verily I say unto you they have joy in their works for a season, and by and by the end cometh, and they are hewn down and cast into the fire, from whence there is no return."

According to his instructions, the Church was called the Church of Jesus Christ, just as it is today, after having been restored to the earth in our time.

Before leaving the disciples, the Lord again commanded them to teach the people to repent and live his teachings. He told them that for a time they would be a righteous people, but that when the fourth generation came, the people of that day would be led into sin and destruction.

CHAPTER EIGHTY-NINE

The Three Nephites

III Nephi 28.

*B*EFORE LEAVING them to carry on their ministry, the Savior asked the twelve disciples if they had any wishes they would like him to grant to them.

All but three of the twelve said, "We desire that after we have lived unto the age of man, that our ministry, wherein thou hast called us, may have an end, that we may speedily come unto thee in thy kingdom."

Jesus was willing to grant this request. He said to them, "Blessed are ye because ye desired this thing of me; therefore, after that ye are seventy and two years old ye shall come unto me in my kingdom; and with me ye shall find rest."

He then turned to the other three who had not mentioned any request, and asked, "What will ye that I should do unto you, when I am gone unto the Father?"

These three men had a different desire from that expressed by the other nine, and were afraid to mention it to the Savior. Therefore "they sorrowed in their hearts, for they durst not speak unto him the thing which they desired."

But he said, "I know your thoughts, and ye have desired the thing which John, my beloved, who was with me in my ministry, before that I was lifted up by the Jews, desired of me."

John the Beloved Apostle had desired to live on the earth until the second coming of the Savior, laboring among men all through the centuries, to bring souls to Christ. This was also the desire of the three Nephite disciples to whom the Lord now spoke.

The Savior was pleased. Although he had blessed the other nine, to the three he said, "More blessed are ye, for ye shall never taste of death; but ye shall live to behold all the doings of the Father unto the children of men, even until all things shall be fulfilled according to the will of the Father, when I shall come in my glory with the powers of heaven.

"And ye shall never endure the pains of death; but when I shall come in my glory ye shall be changed in the twinkling of an eye from mortality to immortality; and then shall ye be blessed in the kingdom of my Father.

"And again, ye shall not have pain while ye shall dwell in the flesh, neither sorrow, save it be for the sins of the world; and all this will I do because of the thing which ye have desired of me, for ye have desired that ye might bring the souls of men unto me, while the world shall stand.

"And for this cause ye shall have fulness of joy; and ye shall sit down in the kingdom of my Father; yea, your joy shall be full, even as the Father hath given me fulness of joy; And ye shall be even as I am."

After saying this he touched the other nine with his finger, and then departed from them all.

But the three who were to remain on the earth until the second coming of Christ in the latter days, were blessed by the Lord so that a change came over their bodies, and no one could kill them, nor could they feel pain or sorrow.

They were caught up into heaven and transfigured, and returned to earth to do a great work. They went all over the land of America, preaching to the people and baptizing as many into the Church as would believe.

When the enemies of the Church arrested them, and put them in prison, the walls could not hold them, but fell down by the power of God.

When they were put into deep pits in the earth, the Lord delivered them and wicked people could not dig pits deep enough to hold them.

Three times they were cast into a furnace, and no harm came to them. Twice they were thrown into a den of wild animals, but the animals were tamed, so that the disciples could play with them as a child would play with a lamb.

In later years, when Mormon was compiling all of the records into the book we call the Book of Mormon, these three Nephites appeared to him, and helped him in his work.

It is promised that these same disciples will minister among the Gentiles, as well as the Jews, but they will not be recognized, and no one will know them.

They will remain in this condition, so that they cannot die nor feel pain nor sorrow, until the Day of the Lord, when a further change will take place in their bodies and they will be resurrected men. After that, the scripture says, they will be received into the kingdom of the Father, to dwell there with God eternally in the heavens.

CHAPTER NINETY

Two Hundred Years of Peace

IV Nephi.

*T*HE STORMS, earthquakes and other destruction which came during the three days of darkness had completely humbled the people everywhere. Both Nephites and Lamanites had seen the power of God and had seen also how the wicked were destroyed.

As the twelve disciples of the Lord ministered among them, the people welcomed them, and heard their teachings with great joy. Peace prevailed throughout the land. A spirit of brotherhood came among the people. All were willing to help one another.

Those who at first had seen the Savior when he came, were so filled with his Holy Spirit that they divided their property, their food and all their goods, with each other, so that everyone had the same amount. As the rest of the people who had been spared from the great destruction were converted, the same spirit came to them, and they also lived with all things in common.

The Lord blessed and prospered the people, who rebuilt many of the cities which had been destroyed by fire. The cities which had been flooded or crushed by falling mountains, of course could not be rebuilt.

As years went by, death came to each of the nine disciples as they reached their seventy-second year. At last only the three remained who were not to die. They carried on the work, and the Church prospered.

A hundred years passed, with peace in all the land, because the people all lived the gospel. Lamanites and Nephites alike were obedient. They became united as one, and it was not long until no one was called either a Nephite or a Lamanite. All were called the people of God, members of the Church of Jesus Christ. There were no robberies among them, or other crimes, so righteous had the people become.

Another hundred years went by, with continued peace in the land. The people multiplied and became very numerous, so that they spread over large areas, and built many cities.

Being blessed so much for two hundred years, the people became very rich. In the past, riches had led the Nephites into trouble, and so they did again. Some now began to dislike having all things in common. They became vain and selfish, and wished to appear better than others. So they started to wear fine clothing, jewelry, and other costly things. They found many pearls, which were of great value, and they made these into expensive ornaments which they wore.

They would no longer divide their property with others but kept all they had for themselves. They broke away from the main body of the people, rebelled against the Church, and desired to live worldly lives, like so many of their wicked forefathers before them.

They started a church of their own, in which they had doctrines and ordinances of their own making. They did not require the people to repent of their sins, but let them take part in their new church no matter how evil they were. This church began to grow rapidly in membership.

These people then began to persecute the Saints of God. They despised the members of the true Church, in spite of the many miracles which were performed by the prophets of the Lord. They put into prison many of the leaders of the true Church, but the power of the Lord was with these brethren, and at a command, the prisons were shaken down. The brethren then went out and continued to preach and perform many miracles.

The wicked tried to kill them, and especially did they try to kill the Three Nephites who were to remain and not die. They threw them into hot furnaces, and into dens of wild beasts, but could not hurt them.

Two hundred and thirty one years after the coming of the Savior, a great division occurred among the people. All who were faithful to the Church again were known as Nephites, and those who rejected the Church and its teachings were known once more as Lamanites.

These Lamanites taught their children to hate the Nephites, just as the Lamanites had done years before. More and more people joined with them, until the wicked were far more numerous than the righteous.

As time went by, many of the members of the Church also began to sin. Pride came into their hearts, and although they still lived among the Nephites, and did not join the Lamanites, they began to live in sin, so that many of the Nephites became as evil as the Lamanites.

The Three Nephites were deeply grieved at this condition.

By the time three hundred years had passed from the coming of Christ, nearly all of the Nephites were as wicked as the Lamanites.

The Three Nephites saved from fire . .

CHAPTER NINETY-ONE

Mormon, The Boy General

Mormon 1.

*I*N THE DAYS when both the Nephites and the Lamanites had become so wicked, there lived a boy named Mormon, a descendant of the great prophet, Nephi. He loved the Lord and kept his commandments.

Ammaron was the prophet who at this time had possession of all the sacred records which had been handed down from the days of Lehi.

A revelation from the Lord came to Ammaron one day, telling him to hide all of the sacred records in his possession so that the wicked people of his time could not destroy them.

He took the records to a hill called Shim, in a nearby land known to the Nephites as Antum. There he hid them safely, and returned to his home.

Ammaron became acquainted with young Mormon, who at this time was only ten years old. One day he said to Mormon, "I perceive that thou art a sober child, and art quick to observe; therefore, when ye are about twenty and four years old I would that ye should remember the things that ye have observed concerning this people; and when ye are of that age go to the land Antum, unto a hill which shall be called Shim; and there have I deposited unto the Lord all the sacred engravings concerning this people. And behold, ye shall take the plates of Nephi unto yourself, and the remainder shall ye leave in the place where they are; and ye shall engrave on the plates of Nephi all the things that ye have observed concerning this people."

Mormon was impressed with the message of Ammaron, and remembered what the prophet said.

270

About a year later, when Mormon was eleven years old, his father took him southward, to the land of Zarahemla. He saw there that the entire land seemed covered with buildings, and the people "were as numerous almost as it were the sand of the sea."

That year a war broke out in the borders of the land of Zarahemla, between the Nephites and the Lamanites. It was a short war, because the Nephites were much stronger than the Lamanites, and defeated them in several battles. The Lamanites then withdrew from the land occupied by the Nephites, and peace was restored.

The people became more and more wicked, and finally grew so bad that the Lord took from among them his disciples, and from that time there were no more miracles performed there.

When Mormon was fifteen years old, he was visited by the Lord. After that, as a boy, he tried to preach, but because of the widespread wickedness of the people, he was forbidden to go out among them.

When the prophets of the Lord were no more working among the people, the devil tempted them to sin more than ever. Wicked men went about practicing magic, witchcraft and sorcery, and spiritual darkness prevailed.

Although but a boy, Mormon was large of stature. Many of the people knew he was loved of the Lord, and that he was sober and dependable. They wished to have such a man as general of their armies, and even though Mormon then was only sixteen years old, he was chosen as commanding general of the Nephites.

Mormon organized the Nephite soldiers, armed them well, and prepared them to meet the next attack of the Lamanites.

CHAPTER NINETY-TWO

The Nephites Driven North

Mormon 2.

*T*HE LAMANITES planned a great attack upon the Nephites near Zarahemla. Mormon made all preparations to meet them, but they came with such power that the Nephite armies were frightened and refused to fight.

Mormon then led his men into a retreat northward. They came to the city of Angola, which they fortified, for they knew the Lamanites would follow them. In spite of all their preparations, the Nephites could not hold the city, and again had to flee before the Lamanite army.

They went to the land of David, but were driven from there also by the victorious Lamanites. Then they hurried to the land known as Joshua, which was by the west seashore.

While the armies were in Joshua, Mormon sent his men out to gather in all the Nephites from the entire land, and bring them to Joshua, for protection.

But as Mormon saw how wicked they were, he was sad. There were many robbers among them, who stole from each other even in this time of trouble when they might be attacked and slain at any moment by the Lamanite armies.

Many of the Nephites fought among themselves, and would not follow Mormon. But this was true also among the Lamanites, and for a time it seemed that there would be general revolution among all the people.

The Lamanite king at this time was named Aaron. He assembled an army of forty-four thousand, and came against Mormon whose army numbered forty-two thousand. Mormon's army defeated Aaron's, forcing them to flee for their lives.

272

Crime among the Nephites increased. Thieves and robbers stole continually from every one who had any property. There were many murders among the people. The conditions became so bad that the Nephites began to mourn. They loved their riches, and when these were stolen from them, they grieved continually.

At first Mormon believed they were about to repent as he saw their sadness. But he soon found that it was not righteous sorrow. The Lord had withdrawn his spirit from them. They would curse God, and hope to die, and yet they used their weapons to defend themselves when their enemies tried to kill them.

The Lamanites reorganized their forces and called in many more men to strengthen their army. Then they attacked once more, this time driving the Nephites before them.

The fleeing Nephites were not able to stop until they came to the land of Jashon, near where Ammaron had deposited all of the records. Mormon went to the hill Shim, and took from it the plates of Nephi as Ammaron had instructed him. Upon them he wrote a record of all that had happened since the time of Ammaron.

The Lamanites came again. The Nephites fled farther north to the city of Shem, which they hastily fortified. They gathered into that city as many of their people as possible, and hoped they would be safe.

When the enemy came once more, many of the Nephites wished to give up. They were tired of fighting. But Mormon went among them telling what would happen if they surrendered, and commanding them to fight for their wives and their children.

He so encouraged them that when the Lamanite army arrived, the Nephites fought bravely and defeated them in a great battle. As the Lamanites fled, the Nephites chased them, killing as many as they overtook. But even though they won this battle, they knew that the strength of the Lord was not with them, because they were not worthy of it.

The robbers in the land joined forces with the Lamanites, and together they took possession of nearly all of the Nephite cities south of the narrow neck of land. Nothing the Nephites could do seemed to stop the war. At last, tired of battle, they made a treaty with the Lamanites. The treaty gave to the Lamanites the entire country south of the narrow neck of land, and forced the Nephites to move into the land northward, away from their homes and cities and farms. It was a bitter defeat for the Nephites.

CHAPTER NINETY-THREE

Mormon Resigns as General

Mormon 3 and 4.

*T*EN YEARS of peace followed the signing of the treaty with the Lamanites. During this time, Mormon built fortifications, and drilled his people in all the arts of war.

One day the Lord spoke to Mormon, calling him to preach to the people in a last effort to bring them to repentance. "Cry unto this people," the Lord said, "Repent ye, and come unto me, and be ye baptized, and build up again my Church, and ye shall be spared."

Obedient to the Lord, Mormon went among the people and did as he was commanded, but the people would not listen. They did not understand that it was the Lord who had given them this ten year period of peace and had kept the Lamanites from coming against them. They did not realize that it was a time in which to repent, if they would. Instead, they hardened their hearts against God more than before.

At the end of the ten year period, the king of the Lamanites sent a message to Mormon, telling him they were preparing to come against the Nephites again.

Mormon ordered all his people to gather in a city near the entrance to the land southward. They fortified the entrance to the narrow neck of land, thinking that they could keep the Lamanites from invading it.

The Lamanites came and the Nephites beat them back. They stayed away for a year, but came again and were once more beaten by Mormon and his men.

When the Nephites saw that they had beaten their enemies in two successive battles, they began to boast of their own strength, and to swear that they would avenge the blood of their relatives who had been killed by the Lamanites. Their boasting so disgusted Mormon that he now refused to be their leader. He had led them in their victorious battles, and fortified their cities, hoping always that they would repent and turn to the Lord. But with their increased wickedness, he determined not to lead them any more. He would not take part in any of their evil schemes.

The voice of the Lord came to him, saying, "Vengeance is mine, and I will repay; And because this people repented not after I had delivered them, behold they shall be cut off from the face of the earth."

With Mormon no longer as their leader to direct them, the boasting Nephites left their forts and attacked the Lamanites in open country. They were badly defeated. While they were still tired from this bitter battle, another army of Lamanites came upon them, and captured their fortified city near the entrance to the narrow neck of land. Many of the Nephites were either killed or taken prisoners, and the others fled to the city of Teancum which was also near the narrow neck of land.

If the Nephites had remained behind their fortifications, they might have been safe, but they were not strong enough to meet their enemy in the open.

When the Lamanites attacked the city of Teancum, they were driven back. This victory made the Nephites boastful again, and they left Teancum, where they were safe, and marched out against the Lamanite army. The Lamanites continued to retreat, and the Nephites followed them until they came to their first line of forts near the narrow neck of land, and they recaptured them.

As soon as the Lamanites got more reinforcements, they came back once more, defeating the Nephites in their fortresses, driving them back to Teancum, and taking as prisoners many women and children, as well as soldiers.

They killed them and offered them as sacrifices to their idols, for many had become idol worshippers. This so angered the

Nephite soldiers that they attacked the Lamanites in another battle, and fought with frenzy. For a time they were victorious, but because the Lord was no longer with them, they fell back, and from that time on were unable to defeat the Lamanites. It had been prophesied that they would be swept off the face of the land, and now this terrible punishment began to come upon them.

After each victory, the Lamanites took many prisoners and offered them as human sacrifices to their idols.

CHAPTER NINETY-FOUR

Mormon Makes His Book

Mormon 4 and 5 and Words of Mormon.

*A*s THE WARS continued, the Nephites were driven north-ward, and the Lamanites obtained control of the land, Mormon went to the hill Shim, where Ammaron had hidden all the sacred records and took them from their hiding place.

The records had been kept through the thousand years since Lehi had left Jerusalem, and were now numerous. They were kept on many sets of plates.

It was the purpose of the Lord that a synopsis or abridge-ment of all of these records should be written into one book to be brought forth in the latter days, and published to the world.

Mormon was selected to make this abridgement. With great care he engraved upon gold plates a short account of the history of the Nephites from their beginning. He also included the small plates made by the first Nephi, and made them a part of his book. This was for a wise purpose which the Lord had in mind, although that purpose was not made known to Mormon.

Being a prophet of the Lord, Mormon also wrote many of his teachings, and told of the revelations which he himself had received from God.

Mormon had a righteous son named Moroni, and it was his plan at some future time to give the records into his keeping. He also hoped that Moroni would write in the book.

It was this record prepared by Mormon and his son Moroni which became what we know today as the Book of Mormon. This set of gold plates Moroni delivered into the hands of Joseph Smith.

The plates were made of thin sheets of gold, and were held together at the back by a set of rings which permitted the pages to be turned and worked upon.

All of the stories of this book are from the abridgement which Mormon made from the many plates and records which had been handed down to him.

CHAPTER NINETY-FIVE

Mormon Fights Again

Mormon 5-8.

SEEING defeat and disaster coming steadily upon the Nephites, Mormon felt that he should fight again. He went to the leaders of the Nephites and offered his services. They were glad to have him back, and looked upon him as one who could deliver them from all their troubles.

Mormon had little hope of victory, because he knew that the people were not repentant, and therefore God would not spare them.

The Lamanites continued to drive the Nephites before them, burning towns and villages. The Nephites under Mormon fought many times to halt the victorious Lamanites, but they could not stop them.

No longer able to keep them back the Nephites were forced to retreat. All who could not keep ahead of the oncoming enemy were captured by them and killed. The war continued year after year, with the Nephites in retreat, going farther into the land northward.

The Nephites now came into a land known to them as Cumorah, where there was a large hill, which was also called Cumorah. Mormon wrote a letter to the king of the Lamanites, asking for permission to gather all the Nephites upon the Hill Cumorah, where they would give battle to the Lamanites.

The king granted his request, and Mormon and his people marched to the foot of the hill where they pitched their tents. There was much water in the land of Cumorah with lakes, rivers and fountains. Mormon hoped that this would give them some advantage over their enemies.

He gathered all the Nephites to this place, and prepared them for their last great battle.

Mormon was now becoming an old man. He feared for the safety of the records which he had carried with him as his armies retreated before the Lamanites. He did not want them to fall into the hands of wicked men who would destroy them.

Taking all the records which had been entrusted to him, except the plates containing his abridgement, he hid them in the Hill Cumorah. The plates with his abridgement were given to his son Moroni.

He then went back to his task of preparing to meet the Lamanites who were armed with swords, bows and arrows, battle axes and other weapons. As their enemies came toward them, the Nephites were filled with fear. The soldiers had with them their wives and children. They were afraid to die, yet they knew that death was near.

The Nephite armies were divided into several groups, each with ten thousand men. Mormon commanded one force of ten thousand, his son Moroni commanded a similar one, and other leaders of the Nephites each had ten thousand.

Out of all the thousands in the armies of the Nephites, every one was killed that day in the battle on Cumorah except twenty-four. Mormon was severely wounded. Moroni was unhurt. The destruction of the Nephites was almost complete. Some fled into the wilderness, but were hunted down and killed. Some joined the Lamanites to save their lives.

The twenty-four who survived the first day's battle, were later killed by the Lamanites, with the exception of Moroni. He alone was left, the last of the Nephites on the entire land. He remained in hiding, and completed his father's record.

After destroying the Nephites at the Hill Cumorah, the Lamanites went from place to place searching for Nephites who had been left behind as the armies went north. Wherever they found the Nephites they killed them.

Then the Lamanites began to fight among themselves, and many were slain in these battles. Except for Moroni, there remained not one person in the whole of America who believed in God, or knew of Jesus the Christ.

CHAPTER NINETY-SIX

Moroni Writes His Record

Mormon 8 and 9; Moroni 1-7; Ether 12:39.

ORONI took the plates his father had given him, and began to finish the record. He did not know how long he might be allowed to live. He knew that the record must be completed, and hidden up to come forth in the last days.

He described the final scenes of the battles as he saw them, and then recorded certain prophecies about the coming forth of the record in modern times. He knew his writing was not perfect. Therefore he said, "if there be faults, they be the faults of a man."

The Lord gave Moroni visions of the future, and showed him many things which would take place in the last days. He saw that people in our day would wear fine clothes, be proud in their hearts, oppress the poor, and persecute the righteous. He saw that there would be man-made churches, but that the people who attended them would not have the spirit of God.

"Yea, it shall come in a day when there shall be heard of fires, and tempests, and vapors of smoke in foreign lands; and there shall also be heard of wars, rumors of wars, and earthquakes in divers places."

He warned all who would read his record to believe in God, and keep his commandments, and be saved.

Among the records which Moroni studied while he was hiding, was the record of Ether, the story of the Jaredites, who had lived in America before the coming of Lehi and his family. Moroni wrote a short account of that record, and included it in the plates of his father, which now make up the Book of Mormon. It is called the Book of Ether.

The Savior appeared to Moroni and comforted him. Of this he said, "And then shall ye know that I have seen Jesus, and that he hath talked with me face to face, and that he told me in plain humility, even as a man telleth another in mine own language, concerning these things."

Having made the abridgement of the Book of Ether, Moroni had not intended writing more. "But," he said, "I have not as yet perished; and I make not myself known to the Lamanites lest they should destroy me. For behold, their wars are exceedingly fierce among themselves; and because of their hatred they put to death every Nephite that will not deny the Christ. And I, Moroni, will not deny the Christ. Wherefore I wander whithersoever I can for the safety of mine own life.

"Wherefore, I write a few more things, contrary to that which I had supposed; for I had supposed not to have written any more; but I write a few more things, that perhaps they may be of worth unto my brethren, the Lamanites in some future day, according to the will of the Lord."

He then copied into the record the words of the Savior as he chose his twelve disciples or ministers among the Nephites, and explained how priests and teachers were called and ordained in his day.

He also wrote into the record the exact wording which the Nephites used in blessing the sacrament of the Lord's Supper. It is the same as that given by revelation to the Prophet Joseph Smith, which we use in our meetings.

He told of the manner of baptism among the Nephites, and explained that persons were baptized only if they were repentant and determined to serve the Lord for the rest of their lives. All who were baptized were given the gift of the Holy Ghost.

Then he copied some of the writings of his father, Mormon. One of the beautiful things taught by Mormon, and preserved in the writings of Moroni, is this:

"Wherefore, if a man have faith he must needs have hope; for without faith there cannot be any hope.

"And again, behold I say unto you that he cannot have faith and hope, save he shall be meek, and lowly of heart.

"If so, his faith and hope is vain, for none is acceptable before God, save the meek and lowly in heart; and if a man be meek and lowly in heart, and confesses by the power of the Holy Ghost that Jesus is the Christ, he must needs have charity; for if he have not charity he is nothing; wherefore he must needs have charity.

"And charity suffereth long, and is kind, and envieth not, and is not puffed up, seeketh not her own, is not easily provoked, thinketh no evil, and rejoiceth not in iniquity but rejoiceth in the truth, beareth all things, believeth all things, hopeth all things, endureth all things.

"Wherefore, my beloved brethren, if ye have not charity, ye are nothing, for charity never faileth. Wherefore, cleave unto charity, which is the greatest of all, for all things must fail—

"But charity is the pure love of Christ, and it endureth forever; and whoso is found possessed of it at the last day, it shall be well with him."

CHAPTER NINETY-SEVEN
Baptizing Children
Moroni 8.

*B*EFORE Mormon was killed in the last war between the Nephites and Lamanites, he wrote his son Moroni several letters, and these Moroni copied upon the plates.

One of the letters told of the baptism of little children. There were some in those days who taught that babies should be baptized. Mormon knew that this was wrong, and wrote a letter to Moroni about it. Among other things Mormon wrote:

"For, if I have learned the truth, there have been disputations among you concerning the baptism of your little children.

"And now, my son, I desire that ye should labor diligently, that this gross error should be removed from among you; for, for this intent I have written this epistle.

"For immediately after I had learned these things of you I inquired of the Lord concerning the matter. And the word of the Lord came to me by the power of the Holy Ghost, saying:

"Listen to the words of Christ, your Redeemer, your Lord and your God. Behold, I came into the world not to call the righteous but sinners to repentance; the whole need no physician, but they that are sick; wherefore, little children are whole, for they are not capable of committing sin; wherefore the curse of Adam is taken from them in me, that it hath no power over them; and the law of circumcision is done away in me.

"And after this manner did the Holy Ghost manifest the word of God unto me; wherefore, my beloved son, I know that it is solemn mockery before God, that ye should baptize little children.

"Behold I say unto you that this thing shall ye teach—repentance and baptism unto those who are accountable and capable of committing sin; yea, teach parents that they must repent and be baptized, and humble themselves as their little children, and they shall all be saved with their little children.

"And their little children need no repentance, neither baptism. Behold, baptism is unto repentance to the fulfilling the commandments unto the remission of sins.

"But little children are alive in Christ, even from the foundation of the world; if not so, God is a partial God, and also a changeable God, and a respecter to persons; for how many little children have died without baptism!

"Wherefore, if little children could not be saved without baptism, these must have gone to an endless hell.

"Behold I say unto you, that he that supposeth that little children need baptism is in the gall of bitterness and in the bonds of iniquity, for he hath neither faith, hope, nor charity; wherefore, should he be cut off while in the thought, he must go down to hell.

"For awful is the wickedness to suppose that God saveth one child because of baptism, and the other must perish because he hath no baptism.

"Wo be unto them that shall pervert the ways of the Lord after this manner, for they shall perish except they repent. Behold, I speak with boldness, having authority from God; and I fear not what man can do; for perfect love casteth out all fear.

"And I am filled with charity, which is everlasting love; wherefore, all children are alike unto me; wherefore, I love little children with a perfect love; and they are all alike and partakers of salvation.

"For I know that God is not a partial God, neither a changeable being; but he is unchangeable from all eternity to all eternity.

"Little children cannot repent; wherefore, it is awful wickedness to deny the pure mercies of God unto them, for they are all alive in him because of his mercy.

"And he that saith that little children need baptism denieth the mercies of Christ, and setteth at naught the atonement of him and the power of his redemption.

"Wo unto such, for they are in danger of death, hell, and and endless torment. I speak it boldly; God hath commanded me. Listen unto them and give heed, or they stand against you at the judgment-seat of Christ.

"For behold that all little children are alive in Christ, and also all they that are without the law. For the power of redemption cometh on all them that have no law; wherefore, he that is not condemned, or he that is under no condemnation, cannot repent; and unto such baptism availeth nothing."

CHAPTER NINETY-EIGHT

Moroni's Farewell

Moroni 10.

*T*WENTY YEARS after the last great battle, Moroni was still alive, a lone man wandering upon the earth.

He was ready now to seal up the record which he had kept all this time. Before doing so, he wished to write his final testimony about the truthfulness of the Book of Mormon. He said:

"And I seal up these records, after I have spoken a few words by way of exhortation unto you.

"Behold, I would exhort you that when ye shall read these things, if it be wisdom in God that ye should read them, that ye would remember how merciful the Lord hath been unto the children of men, from the creation of Adam even down unto the time that ye shall receive these things, and ponder it in your hearts.

"And when ye shall receive these things, I would exhort you that ye would ask God, the Eternal Father, in the name of Christ, if these things are not true; and if ye shall ask with a sincere heart, with real intent, having faith in Christ, he will manifest the truth of it unto you, by the power of the Holy Ghost.

"And by the power of the Holy Ghost ye may know the truth of all things."

Then he wrote of the gifts of the Holy Ghost, and said:

"And again, I exhort you, my brethren, that ye deny not the gifts of God, for they are many; and they come from the same God. And there are different ways that these gifts are administered; but it is the same God who worketh all in all; and they are given by the manifestations of the Spirit of God unto men, to profit them.

"For behold, to one is given by the Spirit of God, that he may teach the word of wisdom;

"And to another, that he may teach the word of knowledge by the same Spirit;

"And to another, exceeding great faith; and to another, the gifts of healing by the same Spirit;

"And again, to another, that he may work mighty miracles;

"And again, to another, that he may prophesy concerning all things;

"And again, to another, the beholding of angels and ministering spirits;

"And again, to another, all kinds of tongues;

"And again, to another, the interpretation of languages and of divers kinds of tongues.

"And all these gifts come by the Spirit of Christ; and they come unto every man severally, according as he will.

"And I would exhort you, my beloved brethren, that ye remember that every good gift cometh of Christ."

After this he said:

"And I exhort you to remember these things; for the time speedily cometh that ye shall know that I lie not, for ye shall see me at the bar of God; and the Lord God will say unto you: Did I not declare my words unto you, which were written by this man, like as one crying from the dead, yea, even as one speaking out of the dust?"

After bearing his testimony of Jesus the Savior, he closed the book with these words:

"And now I bid unto all, farewell. I soon go to rest in the paradise of God, until my spirit and body shall again reunite, and I am brought forth triumphant through the air, to meet you before the pleasing bar of the great Jehovah, the Eternal Judge of both quick and dead. Amen."

Moroni's farewell

CHAPTER NINETY-NINE

A Prophecy For Our Time

III Nephi 21; II Nephi 29.

*W*HEN JESUS was among the Nephites he prophesied to them that the Book of Mormon records would be given to a modern nation of Gentiles which should live in America in the latter-days. This is what he said:

"For it is wisdom in the Father that they (the Gentiles) should be established in this land, and be set up as a free people by the power of the Father, that these things (the sacred records) might come forth from them unto a remnant of your seed, that the covenant of the Father may be fulfilled which he hath covenanted with his people, O house of Israel.

"Therefore, when these works, and the works which shall be wrought among you hereafter, shall come forth from the Gentiles, unto your seed, which shall dwindle in unbelief because of iniquity; for thus it behoveth the Father that it should come forth from the Gentiles, that he may show forth his power unto the Gentiles, for this cause, that the Gentiles, if they will not harden their hearts, that they may repent and come unto me, and be baptized in my name, and know of the true points of my doctrine, that they may be numbered among my people, O house of Israel.

"And when these things come to pass, that thy seed shall begin to know these things, it shall be a sign unto them, that they may know that the work of the Father hath already commenced unto the fulfilling of the covenant which he hath made unto the people who are of the house of Israel."

Soon after the Nephites came to America, the Lord revealed that not only would the Book of Mormon be given to us in these modern times, but that the lost Ten Tribes would write a similar record, and that it would also be given to us. He said that the

292

writings of the Jews, meaning the Bible, would be given to man-kind, but that these other ancient records would also be published in latter days. This is what he said:

"Behold, I shall speak unto the Jews, and they shall write it; and I shall also speak unto the Nephites, and they shall write it; and I shall also speak unto the other tribes of the house of Israel, which I have led away, and they shall write it; and I shall also speak unto all nations of the earth and they shall write it.

"And it shall come to pass that the Jews shall have the words of the Nephites, and the Nephites shall have the words of the Jews; and the Nephites and the Jews shall have the words of the Lost Tribes of Israel, and the Lost Tribes of Israel shall have the words of the Nephites and the Jews.

"And it shall come to pass that my people which are of the House of Israel, shall be gathered home unto the lands of their possessions; and my word also shall be gathered in one."

The words of the ancient Jews form the Bible; the words of the Nephites are in the Book of Mormon. The writings of the Lost Tribes have not as yet been given to the world.